Putting the Power of Your Subconscious Mind to Work

Titles by Joseph Murphy

THE POWER OF YOUR SUBCONSCIOUS MIND
THE MIRACLE OF MIND DYNAMICS
YOUR INFINITE POWER TO BE RICH
SECRETS OF THE I CHING
THE AMAZING LAWS OF COSMIC MIND POWER
THINK YOURSELF RICH
THINK YOURSELF TO HEALTH, WEALTH & HAPPINESS
PUTTING THE POWER OF YOUR SUBCONSCIOUS MIND TO WORK

Putting the Power of Your Subconscious Mind to Work

Reach New Levels of Career Success
Using the Power of Your Subconscious Mind

Joseph Murphy, Ph.D., D.D.
Compiled and edited by Arthur R. Pell, Ph.D.

PRENTICE HALL PRESS

PRENTICE HALL PRESS
Published by the Penguin Group
Penguin Group (USA) Inc.
375 Hudson Street, New York, New York 10014, USA
Penguin Group (Canada), 90 Eglinton Avenue East, Suite 700, Toronto, Ontario M4P 2Y3, Canada
(a division of Pearson Penguin Canada Inc.)
Penguin Books Ltd., 80 Strand, London WC2R 0RL, England
Penguin Group Ireland, 25 St. Stephen's Green, Dublin 2, Ireland (a division of Penguin Books Ltd.)
Penguin Group (Australia), 250 Camberwell Road, Camberwell, Victoria 3124, Australia
(a division of Pearson Australia Group Pty. Ltd.)
Penguin Books India Pvt. Ltd., 11 Community Centre, Panchsheel Park, New Delhi—110 017, India
Penguin Group (NZ), 67 Apollo Drive, Rosedale, North Shore 0632, New Zealand
(a division of Pearson New Zealand Ltd.)
Penguin Books (South Africa) (Pty.) Ltd., 24 Sturdee Avenue, Rosebank, Johannesburg 2196, South Africa

Penguin Books Ltd., Registered Offices: 80 Strand, London WC2R 0RL, England

While the author has made every effort to provide accurate telephone numbers and Internet addresses at the time of publication, neither the publisher nor the author assumes any responsibility for errors, or for changes that occur after publication. Further, the publisher does not have any control over and does not assume any responsibility for author or third-party websites or their content.

First edition: February 2009

Library of Congress Cataloging-in-Publication Data

Murphy, Joseph, 1898–1981.
    Putting the power of your subconscious mind to work : reach new levels of career success using the power of your subconscious mind / Joseph Murphy ; compiled and edited by Arthur R. Pell.—1st ed.
        p. cm.
    Includes index.
    ISBN 978-0-7352-0436-2
    1. Success in business—Psychological aspects.   2. Success.   3. Attitude (Psychology).
I. Pell, Arthur R.   II. Title.
    BF637.S8M83 2009
    154.2—dc22   2008043020

PRINTED IN THE UNITED STATES OF AMERICA

10   9   8   7   6   5   4   3   2   1

Contents

Introduction:
Understanding the Power of
Your Subconscious Mind vii

Part One

Maximizing the Personal Attributes
That Lead to a Successful Career 1

1. Establishing and Achieving Your Goals 3

2. Developing Self-Confidence and Self-Worth 15

3. Becoming a More Positive Thinker 27

4. Mastering the Law of Attraction 39

5. Becoming a More Enthusiastic Person 51

6. Developing Resilience and Adaptability 59

7. Overcoming Worry and Stress 71

8. Conquering Fear 82

9. Enhancing Your Creative Powers 93

10. Breaking Bad Habits 106

Part Two

Obtaining Cooperation and Support of Others.............. 119

11. Becoming a Leader...121

12. Creating a Dynamic Team...135

13. Expressing Sincere Appreciation..148

14. Communicating More Effectively..160

15. Dealing with Difficult People..173

16. Managing Your Time..187

17. Selling Your Ideas..198

18. Advancing Your Career...211

Index...223

Understanding the Power of Your Subconscious Mind

Whatever your conscious mind assumes and believes to be true, your subconscious mind will accept and bring to pass. Believe in good fortune, divine guidance, right action, and all the blessings of life. You are the captain of your soul (subconscious mind) and the master of your fate. Remember, you have the capacity to choose. Choose life! Choose love! Choose health! Choose happiness!

Are you unhappy in your career? Is your advancement stymied by ostensible lack of opportunity? Do you want to succeed in achieving your goals? You need not be restricted by a dogmatic boss or bureaucratic red tape, or depend on luck or fortuity. You have the power within you to take charge of your career.

All that we achieve as well as all that we fail to achieve is the direct result of our own thoughts. Our weaknesses and strengths, purity and impurity, are ours alone. They can only be altered by *us*; never by another. All our happiness and suffering are evolved from within. *As we think, so we are; as we continue to think, so we remain.*

Of course, there are some things you cannot change: the movement of planets, the change in seasons, the pull of the oceans and tides, and the apparent rising and setting of the sun. *But you can change yourself*. You can be transformed by the renewing of your mind. This is the key to improving your career. Your mind is a recording machine, and all the beliefs, impressions, opinions, and ideas accepted by you consciously are impressed in your deeper, subconscious mind. By learning how to channel your subconscious mind, you can gain control over your career.

Yes, you have the power to change what is in your subconscious mind. It starts by taking overt steps to absorb noble patterns of thoughts. Think thoughts of beauty, love, peace, wisdom, and creative ideas. Your subconscious mind will respond accordingly, transforming your mentality, your body, and the circumstances surrounding your life.

This is especially true when applied to advancing your career. Too many people hinder their career growth by fear—fear of displeasing a boss, fear of rivals in their move up the career ladder, fear of bureaucratic impasses. Yes, any or all of these fears can affect your career, but only if you let them.

If you are confident in your own abilities and work effectively in achieving company goals, you will engage the power of your subconscious mind to overcome all obstacles.

When a large law firm hired Jules H., a bright young attorney, he noticed that there were a dozen young attorneys competing with him for advancement. They were all highly competent and equally ambitious. He noted that most of these associates were constantly complaining about the long hours doing routine detail work instead of the more interesting legal work they all desired. Jules, although equally frustrated, called on the power of his subconscious mind and told himself: "Sure, this work is boring and brain-numbing, but it's the dues I have to pay if I want to get ahead. I will do this work, not just with my brain, but with my heart. I'll deal with it just as I tackled my most challenging assignments in law school." It didn't take long for his bosses to recognize his superiority and to begin assigning him more important cases and move him ahead of his rivals.

Psychologists and psychiatrists point out that when thoughts are conveyed to your subconscious mind, impressions are made in the brain cells. As soon as your subconscious accepts any idea, it proceeds to put it into effect immediately. It works by association of ideas and uses every bit of knowledge that you have gathered in your lifetime to bring about its purpose. It draws on the infinite power, energy, and wisdom within you. It lines up all the laws of nature to get its way. Sometimes it seems to bring about an immediate solution to your difficulties, but at other times it may take days, weeks, or longer.

Your subconscious mind is like the soil, which accepts any kind of idea—good or bad. Your thoughts are active and might be likened to seeds. Negative, destructive thoughts continue to work negatively in your subconscious mind and in due time will evolve into actions that correspond with them. Remember, your subconscious mind does not engage in proving whether your thoughts are good or bad, true or false. But it responds according to the nature of your thoughts or suggestions.

For example, if you consciously assume something to be true, even though it may be false, your subconscious mind will accept it as true and proceed to bring about results that must necessarily follow if it were true. Your subconscious mind cannot argue controversially. Hence, if you give it wrong suggestions, it will accept them as true and will proceed to bring them to pass as conditions, experience, and events. Your subconscious mind is often referred to as your subjective mind. Your subjective mind takes cognizance of its environment by means independent of the five senses.

Your subjective mind perceives by intuition. It is the seat of your emotion and the storehouse of memory. Your subjective mind performs its highest functions when the objective mind is suspended or in a sleepy, drowsy state. Your subjective mind sees without the use of the natural organs of vision. It has the capacity of clairvoyance and clairaudience.

When your conscious and subconscious minds function harmoniously and peacefully, the result is harmony, health, peace, joy, and happiness. All the evil, pain, suffering, misery, war, crime, and sickness in the world are due to the inharmonious relationship of the conscious and subconscious mind. Remember, your subconscious is impersonal and nonselective.

The habitual thinking of your conscious mind establishes deep grooves in your subconscious mind. This is very favorable for you and your career if your habitual thoughts are harmonious, peaceful, and constructive.

On the other hand, if you have indulged in fear, worry, and other destructive forms of thinking, the remedy is to recognize the omnipotence of your subconscious mind and decree freedom, happiness, perfect health, and prosperity. Your subconscious mind, being creative and one with your divine source, will proceed to create the freedom and happiness that you have earnestly decreed.

Chance or accident are not responsible for the path your career takes; nor is predestined fate the author of your fortune or misfortune. Your subconscious mind is not concerned with the truth or falsity of what you consciously feel or believe to be true. Select only that which is true, lovely, noble, and Godlike; and your subconscious will react accordingly.

Although philosophers, theologians, and thinkers throughout the ages knew this, each generation must be reminded of this and make it work for its members.

Dr. Joseph Murphy, in his bestselling book, *The Power of Your Subconscious Mind,* and his subsequent writings synthesized this concept. Thousands of men and women came to the sermons and lectures he presented in dozens of countries, and millions listened to his radio broadcasts.

Dr. Murphy converts these theories into practical approaches to life. He provides a no-nonsense program that will teach you how to stop condemning yourself. You will be shown that you can now claim what you want to be. You can now possess what you long to possess. You can now do what you long to do. You can live in that mental atmosphere. It will gradually sink down by osmosis from your conscious to your subconscious, gradually becoming a conviction as you nourish it and sustain it. Then your limitations will disintegrate and you will rise like the phoenix from the ashes of the old and become the new person.

You will acquire a new vision, a new image of yourself, a new awareness. It's your deep-seated beliefs, your emotional espousals, that govern you and control you. Whatever idea or belief is dominant in your subconscious mind takes control of your thoughts, your actions and reactions. If you believe in failure, you cannot succeed. You could work eighteen hours a day, work very hard; but you still would fail because that's the dominant idea in your mind. According to your belief, it will be done unto you. It's a science of the mind.

You will learn how to expect the best, to look forward with anticipation to a most glorious future, to believe it is possible. With this new image of yourself, you will experience the joy and thrill of the fulfillment of your dream. You will learn how to apply these principles to develop and advance in your job and your career.

Although the contents of this book is drawn primarily from Dr. Murphy's works, it has been augmented with additional information and examples to illustrate how valuable its message is to the readers of the twenty-first century.

As Dr. Murphy was a minister, many of his suggestions are based on his strong belief in God. However, whether you are religious, agnostic, or an atheist, you can experience this Infinite Intelligence functioning for you. You need no creed. If you will call upon It, It will answer you. It's impersonal, no respecter of persons. To religious people, this Infinite Intelligence is God. To others it may be considered to be something deep within oneself. You can call it Superhuman Intelligence, if you want to, or the subliminal mind.

If you have a problem—mental, physical, or emotional—that is holding you back at work, ask yourself: What am I turning away from? What is it I don't want to face? Am I hiding my resentment and hostility to someone? Face the problem. Solve it with the knowledge of your deeper mind, knowing that the Life Principle always seeks to heal, to restore. The Life Principle is the vital force that animates us. It never condemns. It never punishes. It never judges. It can't. You pass judgment on yourself by your own thought, the conclusion, verdict, in your own mind. Remember, the Life Principle cannot punish you. It cannot judge you. You judge yourself. And you mold and you fashion your own destiny, for as you think in your heart or subconscious so are you.

Realize, therefore, that thoughts are things; what you feel you attract; what you imagine you become. Then wonders will begin to happen in your life if you do that. Because there's only One Power and that Power is within you. You are the captain on the bridge; you are giving the orders, and your subconscious mind will take the impression you give it and bring it to pass, whether it's true or not, as we said. Therefore, accept only those things that are true.

Our minds are cluttered up with false beliefs, ideas, and opinions; and are opaque with these eternal truths. Suggestions of fear made to a person full of confidence and faith have absolutely no effect. They reinforce faith and confidence in the principle of success. They reinforce the concept that the Infinite can't fail, and suggestions of failure simply result in that person's having greater confidence in his or her inner powers.

Innumerable experiments by psychologists and psychiatrists and others on persons in the hypnotic state have shown that the subconscious mind is incapable of making selections and comparisons, which are necessary for a reasoning process.

You must realize that your conscious mind is your sentry at the gate. Its chief function is to protect your subconscious mind from false impressions. You are now aware of one of the basic laws of mind: Your subconscious mind is amenable to suggestion. As you know, your subconscious mind does not make comparisons or contrasts; neither does it reason or think things out for itself. This latter function belongs to your conscious mind. It simply reacts to the impressions given to it by your conscious mind. It does not show a preference for one course of action over another.

Remember that a suggestion cannot impose something on the subconscious mind against the will of the conscious mind. Your conscious mind has the power to reject any false or negative suggestion.

You must make certain to give your subconscious mind only suggestions that heal, bless, elevate, and inspire you in all your ways. Remember that your subconscious mind takes you at your word. It takes you literally. If you keep saying, "I can't get that promotion, I can't make ends meet," your subconscious will see to it that you can't.

Another influence on your subconscious is suggestions from another person. The power of suggestion has played a part on human life and thought in every period of time, in each country of the earth. In many parts of the world it is the controlling power of religion, with constant reiteration of such comments as "You are a sinner," "The Devil is going to get you," "When you die you are going to go to hell," and things of that nature. It frightens the life out of people.

From infancy on, the majority of us have been given many negative suggestions. Constructive suggestions, of course, are wonderful and magnificent. A negative suggestion, however, is one of the most destructive of all of the response patterns of the mind, resulting in war, misery, suffering, racial and religious prejudices, and disaster. The dictators, despots, and tyrants of the world know the power of suggestion. Stalin practiced it; Hitler practiced it; Osama bin Laden practiced it, appealing to the religious and racial prejudices of people; then when they were highly emotionally aroused, planting more negative suggestions, repeating certain things over and over again to millions of these people.

You are exposed to negative suggestions in all aspects of your life. Here are some frequently heard ones that relate to your job and career: "You can't," "You'll never amount to anything," "You mustn't," "You'll fail," "You haven't got a chance," "You're all wrong," "It's no use," "It's not what you know but who you know," "What's the use?" "Nobody cares," "It's no use trying so hard," "You're too old now," "Things are getting worse and worse," "Life is an endless grind," "You just can't win," "Pretty soon you'll be fired," "You can't trust a soul."

These are commands to your subconscious mind, which will cause your life to be a living hell. You'll be frustrated, neurotic, inhibited. You'll haunt the psychiatrist's office, because you are giving these destructive suggestions to yourself.

You can reject all these negative suggestions by feeding your subconscious mind with prayer, or reading an inspirational meditation before you go to sleep. This will counteract all these destructive ideas.

You don't have to be influenced by destructive negative suggestions. If you look back, you can easily recall how parents, friends, relatives, teachers, bosses, and clergy contributed in a campaign of these destructive suggestions. The purpose of much of it was to control you or instill fear into you. You will find that many of these suggestions are for the purpose of making you think, feel, and act as others want you to, and to take the road that is to their own advantage.

You are not another person's puppet. You must choose your own road, the road that leads to wholeness, the path of freedom. That path is within you. Whatever you decide to be true in your conscious mind you will experience with your subconscious mind. Therefore, believe that God, or Infinite Intelligence, is guiding you. Right action reigns supreme. Divine law and order governs you.

Divine peace fills your soul. Begin to believe in all these things. You don't create these things, but you activate them; make them potent in your life.

Do your own thinking. You have the power to control your own emotions. In your job and career, it is you, not your bosses or coworkers, who must have control over your destiny.

Be inspired from on high. As you accept these truths with your conscious mind, your subconscious will bring all these things to pass, and you will discover that you are not being held back in reaching your goals, that you are moving in the direction you have chosen in your career and in your life.

We must believe we can improve our lives. A belief—whether it is true, false, or merely indifferent—sustained over a period of time becomes assimilated and is incorporated into our mentality. Unless countermanded by belief of an opposite nature, sooner or later it takes form and is expressed or experienced as the fact, form, condition, circumstance, and events of life. We have the power within us to change negative beliefs to positive ones and thereby change our lives for the better.

—Arthur R. Pell, Ph.D.
Editor

PART ONE

Maximizing the Personal Attributes That Lead to a Successful Career

Some are born great, some achieve greatness, and some have greatness thrust upon them.

—SHAKESPEARE, *Twelfth Night*

Although some people may have success thrust upon them, most often, to achieve success, we must take overt steps. Unfortunately, too many people do not recognize the power within them to move out of an unhappy situation and begin climbing the ladder of success.

Within each of us are latent powers that we are not using, but which are waiting to be activated. We may lack self-confidence or self-esteem. We may live in a constant state of worry or fear. We may face unexpected and seemingly insurmountable obstacles in our careers or other aspects of our lives. Many of us have dead-end jobs or just hate to get up each morning to go to an unrewarding, unpleasant work environment. We would like to change, but feel incapable of doing so.

You can change your life. The tools to do this are lodged within you. All you have to do is hone them, use them, and see the results.

In the following chapters we will explore the personal attributes that lead to success and explore how, by channeling the powers of your subconscious mind, you can accelerate your journey to a successful career.

Chapter One

Establishing and Achieving Your Goals

You must give to receive. If you give mental attention to your goals, ideals, and enterprises, your deeper mind will back you up.

All successful people start with a goal. Establishing goals and working toward their achievement is the first step one must take on the long road to success. By knowing where you are going and how you plan to get there, you will be able to focus your time, energy, and emotion—and start on the right track toward reaching those goals.

A ship that has broken its rudder may keep everlastingly at it, may keep on a full head of steam, driving about all the time, but never arrive anywhere. It never reaches any port unless by accident; and if it does find a haven, its cargo may not be suited to the people, the climate, or the conditions. The ship must be directed to a definite port, for which its cargo is adapted, and where there is a demand for it, and it must aim steadily for that port through sunshine and storm, through tempest and fog.

So a person who would succeed must not drift about rudderless on the ocean of life, but must steer straight toward a destined port not only when the ocean is smooth, when the currents and winds serve, but also keep the course in the very teeth of the wind and tempest—even when enveloped in the fogs of disappointment and mists of opposition.

It Starts with a Dream

Do you have a dream—a vision of the future? In your dream are you rich? Famous? Happy? Most people do dream of such a future—but in most cases, that's all it will ever be—a dream.

Successful people have had those dreams, too, but they turned those dreams into goals and in turn into reality. Their dreams were not vague hopes for success, but dreams of specific achievements that they aimed for. Edison dreamed of a world in which electric energy would light up the night. Stephenson dreamed of an engine that would pull trains and eliminate the backbreaking labor of men and beasts. Beethoven dreamed of music that would make the spirit soar. Great actors, artists, musicians, writers dreamed—not just of fame, but of the way they would utilize their talents to achieve success.

Dreaming is not limited to such geniuses. All successful people report that their success started with a hope, a dream. Over the years hundreds of men and women have reported that their achievements all started with a dream, which led to a goal, which led to a plan of action and inevitably to accomplishing the goal.

Dreaming is not limited to the young. It is never too late to have a new dream that leads to new goals that lead to new successes. It is astonishing what people who have had their dreams late in life have accomplished. Benjamin Franklin was past fifty before he began the study of science and philosophy. Milton, in his blindness, was past the age of fifty when he sat down to complete his epic poem *Paradise Lost*.

Dreaming is not limited to biases and prejudices of the times. For countless years, women have been restricted in what they can attempt to accomplish. Their career goals were once limited to what were considered "female jobs." It took determination and courage to even think about other careers. One example is Elaine Pagels, Princeton professor and bestselling author of books on Gnosticism and early Christianity. She said she was educated at a time when girls were taught not to even consider serious careers. She felt free to follow what she loved; only later discovering she could make a living out of it. Her dream had become her goal.

Today the barriers are gone in most career areas. For example, in most law, medical, and other professional schools in the United States, half or more of the students are women.

In the 1990s and early 2000s, many American companies began to outsource jobs to countries where labor costs were significantly lower. This resulted in the loss of jobs for thousands of people. Some people retired; some gave up, went on welfare, and spent years griping about their misfortune. However, the majority drew on their inner resources and trained for jobs in other fields. Most had to start over at lower wages than in their previous employment, but with renewed energy and enthusiasm they began to once again climb the ladder to success.

Even brains are second in importance to determination. Only those with the strong determination that nothing shall impede them are sure that, with perseverance and grit, they will succeed. Dreams become goals and goals become achievements to those who strive long enough and hard enough.

Most of the things that make life worth living, that have emancipated us from drudgery and lifted us above commonness and ugliness—the great amenities of life—we owe to our dreamers.

Converting Dreams into Goals

Unfortunately, too many dreamers remain just that—dreamers. The dreams remain dreams. To make your dreams come true, you must convert them into goals. Then they are no longer fantasies, but objectives that you can set before you as a road map to success. You must bring to your dreams a purpose, a determination that you will do all that you can to make that dream come true.

A woman who had a dream and converted it into a successful goal is the clothing designer Rachel Roy. Rachel's love for fashion was inspired by the movies she saw as a child. The clothes the women wore on the screen seemed to give them an aura of confidence and success. Rachel dreamed that she could create the same aura for herself and other women, a sophisticated look that would create positive self-esteem.

She and her family went school shopping once a year. She was disturbed by the lack of interesting clothing choices in a local store and was convinced that if she had the opportunity she could create better styles. Her mother told her that this was the job of a buyer. Now she could put a name to her dream: "buyer." At that moment, she said, her dream became her goal—to become a buyer in the fashion field.

Her first job was as a stock clerk. She moved rapidly to assistant manager, to personal shopper, to stylist in various stores. She was soon designing fashions and was on the road to a senior position in her company.

When her husband, Damon Dash, wanted to start an independent clothing line, Rachel had a decision to make—whether or not to leave her own successful career to start over with Damon. She chose to start over, throwing herself into the job, working in every capacity, tracking everything she did to contribute, and involving herself in as many facets of the business as possible. She wanted to make herself irreplaceable. After about six years, she was just about to introduce a new line within the company when Damon sold it. By now Rachel was confident she could run a business herself and formed her own company. Her designs were acclaimed by the industry and today she is considered one of the foremost designers in the fashion industry.

There is an infinite distance between the wishers and the doers. Rachel Roy was more than a dreamer and a wisher. She turned her dream into a goal and worked hard to achieve that goal.

Your Secret Weapon—Your Subconscious Mind

Our subconscious minds have a tremendous power in creating in us the habit of expectancy, of believing that we shall realize our ambition; that our dreams will come true.

The very habit of expecting that the future is full of good things for you, that you are going to be prosperous and happy, that you are going to have a fine family, a beautiful home, a successful career, and are going to stand for something, is the best kind of capital on which to start your life.

You must always try to express the ideal. Your subconscious will respond and the things you would like to come true in your life, whether it be robust health, a noble character, or a superb career, will result. If you visualize these results as vividly as possible and try with all your might to realize them, they are more likely to come true than if you do not.

It is only when desire crystallizes into resolve, however, that it is effective. It is the desire coupled with the vigorous determination to realize it that produces the creative power. It is the yearning, the longing, and the striving together that produce results.

If you wish to improve yourself in any particular way, visualize the quality as vividly and as tenaciously as possible and hold a superior ideal along the line of your ambition. Keep this persistently in your mind until you feel its uplift and realization in your life. You are born to win, to conquer, and to lead the triumphant life. You should be a wonderful success in your chosen work, your relationship with people, and in all other phases of your life.

The clearer your instructions are to your subconscious, the more it can help you. This inner mind responds to your commands much the way sailors manning the engine and controls of an ocean liner respond to the orders of the captain on deck. If the words are precise and unmistakable, then the crew sets about turning the vessel to the ordered direction or increasing its speed exactly as they are told.

But if you as a captain are not sure yourself what you want, then your subconscious mind will get an unclear message and your ship will follow a random, or haphazard, or circular course.

You need to tell your subconscious exactly what you want. You need to direct it to help attain your goals. When you know what your true desire really is, your subconscious mind will propel you unerringly toward it. But it needs to know that you genuinely, fervently, and unwaveringly want this goal, and that you will not forsake it for all the other conflicting and contradictory wishes, notions, and momentary fancies that flit through your mind. In that way you become a positive thinker and are set to meet your goals.

Believe in Your Goals and You Will Achieve Them

Prosperity begins in the mind and is impossible to achieve while the mental attitude is hostile to it. It is fatal to work for one thing and to expect something else, because everything must be created mentally first and is bound to follow its mental pattern.

You cannot become prosperous if you really expect or half expect to remain poor. We tend to get what we expect, and to expect nothing is to get nothing.

When every step you take is on the road to failure, how can you hope to arrive at the success goal? Facing the wrong way, toward the black, depressing, hopeless outlook—even though we may be working in the opposite direction—kills the results of our effort.

Thoughts are magnets that attract things like themselves. If your mind dwells upon poverty and disease, it will bring you poverty and disease. There is no possibility of your producing just the opposite of what you are holding in your mind, because your mental attitude is the pattern, which is built into your life. Your accomplishments are achieved mentally first.

The terror of failure and the fear of coming to want and of possible humiliation *keep multitudes of people from obtaining the very things they desire, by sapping their vitality and incapacitating them, through worry and anxiety, for the effective, creative work necessary to give them success.*

Be an optimist. Develop the habit of looking at everything constructively, from the bright, hopeful side, the side of faith and assurance. Refrain from looking at life with doubt and uncertainty. Acquire the habit of believing the best is going to happen, that the right must triumph. Have faith that truth is bound finally to conquer error, that harmony and health are the reality and discord and disease the temporary absence of it. This is the attitude of the optimist, which will ultimately reform the world.

Analyze Yourself

There is only one person in the entire world who can set you on the road to success. That person is you.

Before you can determine what goals can get you started on this journey, you must first evaluate yourself. Search deep inside of your mind and pull out from your subconscious what it is you really want out of life and what assets you have that will lead you to reaching that goal.

You must be realistic. You may want to establish a goal that appears desirable, but you may not have the abilities needed to achieve it. You may want to be a movie star or an opera singer, but don't have the talent needed. Your dream career may be in areas that are not feasible for you to attempt. On the other hand, you may have aptitudes and skills that you don't realize you have and which can lead to a satisfying and profitable career.

How can you find out? Look deeply inside yourself. A careful introspection will bring this out. Most adults already know what they can and cannot do, what they like and do not like. It may not be obvious, but introspection enables you to go beyond the obvious and think deeply about yourself.

A good example of this is Shonda Rhimes, creator and executive producer of the television shows *Grey's Anatomy* and *Private Practice*. Even as a child she knew that she would become a creative writer. She made up stories and spoke them into a tape recorder before she knew how to write. Her mother encouraged her by transcribing them, hence making them real.

What you have to do is go systematically over your education, previous experience, hobbies, and interests. Look for those aspects of your life in which you have been successful and in which you achieved satisfaction and joy. These are indicators of the areas in which you will succeed in the future. But this is only the beginning.

Successful people learn at the very outset of their careers just what funds they can draw upon. Take an inventory of all your possible assets and resources. Don't just look at what you have accomplished thus far in your life, but what you know you can accomplish. The great majority of young people start on their careers with little knowledge of their mental capacities and they usually discover them piece by piece over time.

Most people never discover more than a small percent of their ability and never rise above low-paid, low-level positions. They plod along in mediocrity, yet they have resources; if they could only detect them, it could lift them into superior positions. Somehow they never come in touch with the right sort of ambition-arousing environment or do not come in contact with just the necessary material to ignite the giant power of the *great within* of themselves.

One way to identify your hidden potential is to list those aspects of your schooling, jobs held, and other activities in which you have been engaged. Then reflect on which of these activities you enjoyed doing most, which gave you the most satisfaction, and those you really disliked performing.

Josh D., a twenty-five-year-old college grad, had been very unhappy in his job as a claims adjuster in an insurance company. He had majored in business management and had taken this job with the hope it would lead to a management position. When he listed all the types of activities he performed, he realized that what he liked least was doing detail work. He noted that his boss and his boss's boss spent most of their time in similar activities. He also noted that the aspect of this job that he enjoyed most was dealing with the policyholders, interviewing them and working with them on their claims. In reviewing his school activities and his work with a community group, he found that his most rewarding work had been with people. Josh discussed this with the human resources department of his company, and they suggested he might find his niche and be more successful in a sales position. He made the change and now is enjoying his work and is on the road to a successful career.

Oneness of Purpose

Successful people strongly believe that one must be totally committed to one's goals. There is great power in a resolution that has no reservation in it—a strong, persistent, tenacious purpose that burns all bridges behind it, clears all obstacles from its path, and arrives at its goal, no matter how long it may take, no matter what the sacrifice or the cost.

To succeed you must concentrate all the faculties of your mind upon one unwavering aim, and have tenacity of purpose, which means death or victory. Every other inclination that tempts you must be suppressed.

A one-talent person who decides upon a definite object accomplishes more than a ten-talent person who scatters energies and never knows exactly what to do. By concentrating powers upon one thing, the weakest living creature can accomplish something; by dispersing powers over many things, the strongest may fail to accomplish anything.

A thimbleful of powder behind a ball in a rifle will do more for execution than a carload of powder unconfined. The rifle barrel is the purpose that gives aim to the powder, which otherwise, no matter how good it might be, would be powerless.

It is the single aim that wins. People who succeed have a program. They plan a course and adhere to it. They lay out their plans and execute them. They go straight to their goal. They are not pushed this way and that way every time a difficulty is thrown in their path; if they can't go over it, they go through it. Constant and steady use of faculties under a central purpose gives strength and power, while the use of faculties without an aim or end only weakens them. The mind must be focused on a definite end, or like machinery without a balance wheel, it will rack itself to pieces.

Sum and Substance

Developing goals that are reasonable and achievable is the first step to success—whether it is in your career or any other aspect of your life. You must plant the seeds in your subconscious mind that will enable you to accept and implement these goals. Here are seven steps that will facilitate this process:

1. *Goals should be clearly stated.* Indicate in clear terms what you wish to accomplish. Be specific and firm in stating the goal. For example, saying, "My goal is to be the best salesperson in my company" sounds good, but it is better to be more specific: "My goal is to reach a sales volume of so many dollars for the next fiscal year; and 10 percent more each year for the next three years." Now you know your target, and

your subconscious mind will help concentrate your efforts on reaching those figures.

2. *Goals should be inspiring.* If you set a goal that is too easily attained, it will not motivate you to do more than minimal work. Set goals that will inspire you to keep moving ahead and to work that much harder to achieve them. Achievers recognize that once a goal is reached, they should immediately set another goal that will make them stretch to continue to improve and grow.

3. *Goals should be measurable.* It is not always possible to quantify your goals. Some goals can be measured in financial or other numerical terms. You can set sales figures that you wish to attain by the month, quarter, or year—in terms of units of product or dollar value. You can set production goals by amount. Even intangible goals, which cannot be quantified, can be established in measurable terms. The major goal can be broken into segments and timetables set for the completion of each segment. In this way you can measure how close you are in reaching each of the segments and fine-tune your activities to assure that they will be accomplished in a timely manner.

4. *Goals should be action based.* Unless the actions that will be taken to implement the goals are noted, the goals are no more than dreams. Action requires activity—mental, physical, and emotional. Mentally, you must be prepared to think about your goals every spare moment and what actions you must take to realize them. Your subconscious mind will help you convert your thoughts into actions.

5. *Goals should be written down.* One way to assure that goals will not be forgotten or lost in your hectic day-to-day life is

to write them down. Make a list of your long-term goals; break them into intermediate and short-term goals. Write them in large letters and post them where you can see them every day—over your desk, on the refrigerator, on your mirror. Read them, memorize them, reread them and ask each day: "What am I doing to accomplish these goals?"

6. *Goals should be shared with another person.* Another way of assuring that you will not let your goals go the way of New Year's resolutions is to tell somebody about it—somebody you respect; somebody whom you listen to. Bill Wilson, one of the founders of Alcoholics Anonymous, reported that one of the major acts that help participants in keeping sober is sharing their goals with others. Jean Nidetch, founder of Weight Watchers, reported similar experience.

7. *Goals should be flexible.* There are times when circumstances change and the goal you set is no longer pertinent. Economic conditions may not be favorable for starting that new enterprise; technological innovations may have made your goal obsolete; you have made errors in your research and the goal is not feasible. This does not necessarily mean the goal must be abandoned. It may just require new thinking or more study. If you are faced with such a situation, review what has transpired and make necessary adjustments.

Chapter Two

Developing Self-Confidence and Self-Worth

If you think of yourself as a failure and picture yourself as a failure, you will fail. Think of success. Realize you are born to succeed and to win. Picture yourself successful, happy, and free; and you will be. Whatever you think and feel is true in your conscious mind is embodied in your subconscious and comes to pass into your experience. That's the law of mind, undeviating, immutable, timeless, and changeless. Have faith and you will overcome all obstacles.

There may be countless reasons why one person is successful in his or her career or business and another is not. Over the many years that I have interacted with people—rich and poor, famous and average, leaders and followers—I have observed that the one most significant ingredient that predestines a person to success or lack of success is how one feels about oneself. Those who truly love themselves, who feel that they are people of value, are far more likely to achieve success in their lives than those who lack this belief.

What is it that successful people possess that others may not? It is self-esteem or self-confidence. They believe in themselves and the powers within them.

Self-Esteem—The Basic Ingredient of Self-Confidence

Self-esteem is best defined as feeling good about oneself. People with high self-esteem believe that they are more likely to succeed in most things they do. They respect themselves and know that other people respect them. This does not mean that they are always optimistic about everything and are always cheerful and smiling. We all have bad days and experience times when everything seems to go wrong. People with high self-esteem can accept this and not let it overwhelm them.

Self-esteem is an integral part of self-confidence. Before you can feel good about the decisions you make, you must believe in yourself. You must truly feel that you are someone of worth. If you do not have self-esteem, how can you be *confident* that your decisions are worthwhile?

Why do people lack self-confidence? One common reason is that they may have failed in some activity early in their lives and fear this will happen again. Another is that other people—often teachers or even their own parents—were never satisfied with their performance in school or other matters and have left them with a feeling of inferiority.

Still others have tasted success only to have it followed by some sort of failure and have let that failure dominate their minds and doom them to a lack of self-confidence in anything they do.

The key to changing your feelings about yourself lies in your subconscious mind. The only way for you to reach your subconscious mind is through your conscious mind. Your subconscious is always controlled by the dominant idea. Your subconscious will accept the stronger of two contradictory propositions. If you say, "I want self-confidence but I can't get it; I try so hard; I force myself to pray; I use all the willpower I have," you must realize that your error lies in your effort.

Some people try to exert "willpower" to change their ways. Willpower is an overt attempt to do this. To achieve results you must remove thoughts of the negative from the subconscious, and willpower only reinforces those thoughts. You cannot compel the subconscious mind to accept your idea by exercising willpower. Such attempts are doomed to failure and you get the opposite of what you pray for. When you concentrate on willpower, you only reinforce in your subconscious mind the act you are trying to overcome. For example, when a smoker, trying to break the habit, uses willpower, he or she keeps repeating, "I will not smoke." The subconscious mind then focuses on the act of smoking. If, instead, the smoker concentrates on the joys of freedom from smoking—breathing clean, fresh, odor-free air, and other benefits—the subconscious mind responds accordingly.

If you substitute positive thoughts in your conscious mind to replace the negative ones, they will filter down into the subconscious.

Never Consider Yourself a Failure

It is your estimates, your blueprints, and your beliefs about yourself that govern you. It is not some other person's belief about you. If someone says to you, "You're a failure; you'll never amount to anything," what should you do? Say to yourself, "What another person says about me is irrelevant. I'm born to win, to succeed. I must succeed. I'm going to succeed in a remarkable and unique way."

Every time any person says you are going to fail, it's a stimulus to you to reinforce your faith in the power of your subconscious mind, which never fails. In other words, don't blame others for your failures. Don't blame conditions. Successful people work to overcome poor conditions. Sure, there will be failures, but that does not mean that *you* are a failure. You have within you the creative power to reverse failure, to move on to success. The other person doesn't control you. The power isn't in the other person to manipulate you unless you permit it.

Self-esteem grows within you with each success you have. Self-esteem will even grow when you meet occasional failure if you remember that the power is still with you and you believe in it and have proven it by your actions.

You are what you think you are. You create yourself in the image you have of yourself in your own mind. Self-esteem and self-confidence are nothing more than the projection of your image of yourself. If you maintain a strong positive self-image, you will be a happier and more successful person. You will be a person able to hurdle over roadblocks—no matter how difficult—and achieve the goals you set for yourself.

Your greatest need is to believe in yourself, in what you are doing, and in your ultimate destiny. Self-reliance, or self-confidence, finds its greatest outlet when it is accompanied by a belief that your real self is God-given and that with God all things are possible.

Make up your mind now, this minute. You can have what you wish to possess; and it will be done unto you, as you believe. Follow the age-old maxim: Be sure you are right, then go ahead. Let nothing move you or shake your conviction. Make it a part of your mentality. And with this kind of belief you will inevitably succeed and move forward in life.

Create a Positive Script for Your Life

Psychologists tell us that each of us creates a "script" for our lives. This script may be one of optimism or one of pessimism, one that makes us happy or makes us troubled, one that reflects positive attitudes and self-esteem or one in which negativism dominates our lives, perhaps even self-loathing. Men and women who experience failures early in their careers are subject to a loss of self-esteem and self-confidence. Their early failures affect their psyches. They may subconsciously write for themselves a script of failures—and they *will be* failures unless they can renew their faith in themselves.

If you have written a script of failure, it will dominate your thoughts and actions. You will always consider yourself a failure and you *will* be a failure. Unless you rewrite that script, you are doomed to lifelong failure and unhappiness.

Most successful men and women were not born with success implanted in their genes. Stories of these great people often show how they had to overcome poverty, depression, and what appeared to be overwhelming odds before they reached their goals.

They did this by rewriting their mental scripts and changing their self-image from negative to positive. Then by determination, dedication, and hard work, they began to live the success they had scripted.

Nobody could have started lower in life than Frederick Douglass. He was born a slave on a cotton plantation. As far as opportunity for self-improvement or self-betterment was concerned, he was in about as hopeless and friendless a condition as any person could be. Supposing when he awoke to a realization of his bondage and the hopelessness of his condition, he had said to himself, "Here I am, a slave. No matter how ambitious I may be, or how anxious to get out of this environment, there is no possibility of my doing so, because I was born in slavery. My parents are slaves, and my grandparents were slaves. There is no chance for me to get an education or to get a start in the world outside of this plantation."

If he had reasoned this way with himself, would Frederick Douglass ever have been heard from? Of course he wouldn't. He would have lived and died, even as millions of his fellow bondsmen did, a slave. But he had the will to victory. Instead of saying, "I can't and I won't," he said, "I can and I will work myself out of this horrible condition of slavery."

He wrote a script for himself, calling on the mysterious power latent in every human being that always responds to our call, and conquered all of the apparently insuperable obstacles that stood between him and freedom and education. He learned the alphabet from posters on fences, from scraps of printed paper, and from an old almanac he had picked up on the plantation. He never saw a real book until after he had learned to read.

From such small beginnings, in such an iron environment, this slave boy managed to gain his freedom and secure an education. He made an international reputation for himself as the champion of his enslaved race, to whose cause he devoted his life. His work brought him to the attention of the President of the United States, who appointed him as ambassador to Haiti.

You, too, can rewrite the script that is keeping you mired at the bottom of life's pit. It takes dedication and never-ending effort, but if you want to climb out of that pit, you can, indeed you must, do it.

Some steps to take:

- *Love yourself*. Unless you truly respect yourself, you cannot expect others to love and respect you.

- *Trust yourself*. Don't hesitate to make decisions about your life. If you set your goals and have confidence that you will succeed, you need not fear making decisions that will help you reach those goals.

- *Accentuate the positive*. Sure, you may have some failures along the way, but don't dwell on them. Focus on the achievements you make day by day and your script of success will be reinforced. Self-esteem is perishable. It must be constantly nourished and reinforced. It is nourished by words, by deeds, by attitudes, and by experience, and by your own commitment you maintain it.

- *Demand a great deal from yourself*. When you achieve a small success, congratulate yourself, but this is not the time to become complacent. Use small successes as incentives to seek even higher achievements.

- *Repeat to yourself the adage made famous by the French philosopher Emile Coué:* "Every day, in every way, I am getting better and better."

Give Yourself a Pep Talk

There are times when we need to bolster our self-esteem. Emulate the coach of an athletic team. When the team is falling behind, the coach reaches out to motivate the team—he or she gives them a pep talk. With well-chosen words, the coach instills enthusiasm, self-confidence, and not just the desire to win, but also the commitment to put all their efforts into reaching the goal.

As individuals, we need pep talks, too. We need pep talks when our enthusiasm for life wanes, when we are depressed, when we have suffered failures. When our self-confidence fades and our faith in ourselves is shaken. But where's the coach?

We must be our own coaches. To change the script in your mind, give yourself a pep talk. Tell yourself you are good, you are a winner, you have succeeded in the past, and you will succeed again. By giving yourself a pep talk, you are planting seeds of self-esteem in your conscious mind, which when repeated over and over again will seep into your subconscious mind and become the roots of your behavior.

This self-esteem follows us throughout our lives. In our youth it pushes us forward, in our middle years it sustains us, and in our late years it renews us.

Make it a practice to replace those negative words in your personal script with positive words. Instead of words of despair, plant words of hope; instead of words of failure, create words of success; instead of words of defeat, think words of victory; instead of words of worry, add words of encouragement; instead of words of apathy, plant words of enthusiasm; instead of words of hate, use words of love. Replace all negative words with words of self-esteem and just as day follows night, self-esteem and confidence will permeate your life.

Meet and Beat Obstacles

Self-confidence can be shaken when faced with setbacks. Plans go wrong, unexpected obstacles develop, and everything seems to be collapsing. Now is the time to renew your faith in yourself. Now is the time to call up all the reserves God has given you and meet and beat the problem. You will succeed, and in that success you will enhance your self-esteem.

The best executives commonly agree that the bigger the obstacle, the more self-confidence is demanded and the more valuable the experience is. Early in his career, A. G. Lafley, who became the CEO of Procter & Gamble, was in charge of the company's Asian operations during a major Japanese earthquake and the Asian economic collapse. He said that he managed to lead his company through these formidable obstacles by never losing faith in himself and by keeping in mind that one learns ten times more in a crisis than in normal times.

Similarly, Jeff Immelt, who is now the CEO of General Electric (GE), was put on the spot in a crisis. In 1988 when millions of refrigerator compressors were found to be faulty, CEO Jack Welch put him in charge of fixing the situation even though Immelt had no prior experience with refrigerators or recalls. He said there's no way he'd be CEO today if he hadn't had the confidence in his ability to deal with that "impossible" job, a situation many in GE saw as an insurmountable obstacle.

Another example of overcoming a serious obstacle is that of Cisco CEO John Chambers. He is well known as one of the most dynamic, electrifying speakers in the entire business world. He memorizes just enough of his presentation to have it seem off-the-cuff. He leaves the podium to address people personally. He never loses eye contact with his audience. He is an onstage wizard whose speeches the tough business press characterizes as "aston-ishing."

It is hard to believe that this articulate man had to overcome major obstacles to give him the self-confidence to get up before an audience.

And what gave him this self-confidence? *The power he gained from having to overcome dyslexia.* In order to manage speaking to audiences at all, Chambers had to develop a Spartan work ethic. Instead of complaining about it, he used the challenge to transform himself. He has said his dyslexia forced him to see the big picture instead of being mired in details. This has helped his speaking, be-cause audiences are often bored with details. His dyslexia also forces him to memorize major sections of his presentations and to prepare more diligently than most, giving his presentations a rare kind of immediacy and freshness. When memorized material is presented with liveliness, it's anything but rote, and the opposite of words read from a page. John Chambers is not just a survivor of a damaging childhood handicap. He did not let his handicap domi-nate his life. He worked hard to develop self-confidence, and as a result, he is a business leader who speaks with conviction and clar-ity about people's dreams, the value of his products, and the Big Picture we all want to see.

Stop Punishing Yourself

What you accept completely in your mind, you will get in your experience regardless of condition, circumstances, or the powers that be. Affirm these truths: Promotion is yours, success is yours, right action is yours, wealth is yours. As you do this, these truths will be deposited in your subconscious mind, the creative medium, and wonders will happen in your life.

A legal secretary complained to her pastor: "I never get the breaks. The boss and the other people in the office are mean and cruel to me. My relatives have mistreated me at home all my life.

There must be some kind of a jinx following me. I'm no good. I should jump in the lake."

Her pastor explained to her that she was mentally cruel to herself and that her self-flagellation and self-pity must have substantiation and confirmation on the external plane of life. If you are mean to yourself, other people are going to be mean to you wherever you go in this universe. If you think you're a worm, everybody is going to step on you. In other words, the attitudes and actions of those around her attested to and confirmed her inner state of mind.

She thereupon immediately ceased punishing herself. She pictured herself being congratulated by her employer for very efficient work. She also imaged him announcing an increase in salary for her. She constantly diffused love and goodwill to her employer and to all her associates. Having faithfully sustained her mental image many times a day for several weeks, she was completely dumbfounded when her employer not only congratulated her on her work, but also, some months later, promoted her to a management position. In a few hours' time she realized the wonders of the deeper mind. She had found the key that unlocked the treasure-house.

Don't Say "I Can't"; Say "I Will"

Norman Cousins, editor of *The Atlantic Monthly* and author of *Anatomy of an Illness* and *Human Options*, is a living example of how the power of the subconscious mind enables us to release within us our frequently untapped resources.

Cousins was stricken with an illness that almost paralyzed his neck, arms, hands, fingers, and legs. Soon hospitalized, he was diagnosed as suffering from a serious disease of the connective tissues. His doctor told him, "Your chance for full recovery is one in five hundred."

At first, Cousins allowed his doctor and the hospital "to do their thing" on him. Medication was administered; tests were performed—all confirming the diagnosis and negative prognosis.

But Cousins refused to accept his fate. He strongly believed that laughter, confidence, and the will to live had therapeutic value.

Cousins soon formulated a plan for the pursuit of affirmative emotions. His plan drew upon medical resources, human support systems, laughter, and the love of his family. He then walked out of the hospital, secured a room in a hotel, hired his own nurse, and watched funny movies and television programs. Ten minutes of a good, deep belly laugh, he found, would provide him with two or three hours of pain-free sleep—the first in months.

Week by week, Norman Cousins gained strength; year by year, his mobility improved. He firmly believed that his experience was proof of the power of the will to live and the power of self-confidence to release and unleash the enormous powers within our nature. Cousins lived an active and productive life for sixteen more years.

Capitalize on Your Strengths

Confidence is the very basis of all achievement. There is a tremendous power in the conviction that we can do a thing. People who have great faith in themselves are relieved from a great many uncertainties as to whether they are in the right place, from doubts as to their ability, and from fears regarding their future.

Like most people, even if at this moment you may not be a roaring success in life, you probably are really proficient in some of the things you do. You may not be the best performer in your department, but you may have special capabilities in some aspects of the job that will earn you respect. You may not have been as good an athlete as your classmates, but you may have produced some outstanding work in your art class. You may not make as much money as your neighbors, but you can fix anything that is broken in your home—and theirs.

It's human to worry about your weaknesses—and it gives some

people the incentive to improve them, but it makes many people feel inferior. Instead of brooding about what you cannot do well, glorify in your mind the things at which you are really good. The result: Your self-esteem and your self-confidence will grow and propel you forward to success in all your endeavors.

SUM AND SUBSTANCE

If you think of yourself as a failure and picture yourself as a failure, you will fail. Think of success. Picture yourself succeeding.

- Make up your mind now, this minute, that you can do what you want to do and can be what you sincerely want to be, and can have what you wish to possess; and it will be done unto you as you believe.

- Unless you love and respect yourself, you cannot even start to build up that successful self-image. There is no reason to perpetuate a negative self-image. You must create a positive self-image if you want to be a successful person.

- Never think meanly, narrowly, or poorly of yourself or regard yourself as weak, inefficient, diseased. Think of yourself as perfect, complete, whole.

- There are sure to be roadblocks as you move forward in your career. Never lose self-confidence. The road to success is rarely easy. Program your subconscious mind to be ready and able to meet and defeat barriers to reaching your goals.

Chapter Three

Becoming a More Positive Thinker

The law of life is the law of belief. A belief is a thought in your mind.
Do not believe in things to harm or hurt you. Believe in the power
of your subconscious to heal, inspire, strengthen, and prosper you.
According to your belief is it done unto you.

Negatives never accomplish anything. There is no life in a negative, nothing but deterioration, destruction, and death. Negatives are great enemies of success. People who are always talking down everything, who always complain of hard times and bad business, poor health and poverty, attract destructive, negative influences, and neutralize all of their endeavors.

Constructive thought abandons those who are always thinking destructively and using destructive language, because they are thinking nothing kindred with the positive, nothing to attract it. The creative principles cannot live in a negative, destructive atmosphere, and not a single achievement can take place there. So negative people are always on the downgrade, always turning out failures. They lose the power of affirmation, and drift, unable to get ahead.

Negatives Rob You of Your Power

Negatives will paralyze your ambition if you indulge in them. They will poison your life. They will kill your self-confidence until you are a victim of your situation instead of a master of it. The power to do is largely a question of self-faith, self-confidence. No matter what you undertake, you will never do it until you think you can. You will never master it until you first feel the mastery and do the deed in your mind. It must be thought out or it can never be wrought out. It must be a mind accomplishment before it can be a material one.

Too many people let fear thoughts, failure thoughts, dominate their lives. This leads to settling for non-challenging, dead-end jobs, resulting in mediocre incomes, mediocre lifestyles, and minimum satisfaction in their careers. Even when they have constructive, innovative ideas, they are afraid to suggest them. "What's the point?" they think. They're sure to be rejected.

Men and women with positive attitudes don't settle for being "average guys or gals." Fear is replaced with confidence and their careers flourish.

Be Positive in Your Relationships with Others

Be sure that when you hold an evil thought toward another, an unhealthy thought, a discordant thought, a disease thought, a deadly thought, you call, "Halt! About face!" Look toward the sunlight; determine that if you cannot do any good in the world, you will not scatter seeds of poison, the venom of malice and hatred.

On your job and in your life pursuits, always hold kindly thoughts, charitable, magnanimous, loving thoughts, toward everybody. Then you will not depress them, and hinder, but will scatter sunshine and gladness instead of sadness and shadow, help and encouragement instead of discouragement.

When Marisa L. started on her new job, she noted that she was the only African-American in the department. She tried to make friends with her coworkers, but was rebuffed. Not only did they ignore her, but she felt they went out of their way to make life unpleasant for her.

Marisa's first thought was to report this to the human resources department as a violation of their equal employment opportunity policy, but after further consideration she decided to deal with it herself. Instead of taking a defensive position and confronting these women, she chose to take a positive approach. She replaced her resentment with thoughts of understanding their attitude and meditating on how it could be changed. She studied their work habits and went out of her way to share the specialized knowledge for which she had been hired.

Over a relatively short time, she won the respect and in time the friendship of her coworkers and was accepted as "one of the gang."

Develop an Optimistic Attitude

There is no more uplifting habit than that of bearing a hopeful attitude, of believing that things are going to turn out well and not ill; that we are going to succeed and not fail; that no matter what may or may not happen, we are going to be happy.

To enhance the enjoyment of your job and build relationships that will help you succeed and advance, there is nothing else so helpful as the carrying of this optimistic, expectant attitude—the attitude that always looks for and expects the best, the highest, the happiest—and never allowing oneself to get into a pessimistic, discouraged mood.

Believe with all your heart that you will do what you were made to do. Never for an instant harbor a doubt that you will succeed. Drive it out of your mind if it seeks entrance. Entertain only "thought-friends," ideals of the thing you are determined to achieve.

Reject all "thought-enemies," all discouraging moods, everything that would even suggest failure or unhappiness.

Arianna Huffington, noted television personality and cofounder of the influential online newspaper *Huffington Post*, grew up in Greece. When she was a schoolgirl, she saw a photo of Cambridge University in a magazine and made it known to her family and friends that she wanted to go there. Everybody, most notably her father, said it was clearly a ridiculous idea that should be dropped. But her mother bought cheap airline tickets so she and her determined daughter could visit Cambridge, in order to better visualize Arianna in school there. They met with no school officials or anything like that while they were there; they just walked in the rain and imagined Arianna already in residence there.

Three years later Arianna was accepted by Cambridge University on a scholarship. She says her mother gave her the confidence to always try new things, and that she got the message early that a positive attitude could overcome obstacles. Over the following years Arianna's positive attitude enabled her to achieve success in politics, television, and currently as the publisher of her own online newspaper.

It does not matter what you are trying to do or to be, always assume an expectant, hopeful, optimistic attitude regarding it. You will be surprised to see how you will grow in all your faculties, and how you improve generally.

Two brothers went into business together and were doing fairly well for several years. Then they started to play the futures market and the commodities market and ended up losing everything, including all their business and savings. They owed $50,000, which they were unable to pay, and they went bankrupt.

One brother, who had a very good attitude said, "I have lost money. I will make it again and I will go into business again. I have learned a good lesson, which will ultimately pay me dividends. I have not lost my faith, my confidence, or my ability to rise and grow. I have much to offer and I am going to be a tremendous success again." He went to work for a brokerage firm, and due to his large number of friends, he had no trouble acquiring new accounts for his employer.

His brother, however, felt humiliated and disgraced because he had lost everything. He started telling everyone he met about his losses and monotonously repeated the old refrain that it was his broker's fault, seeking justification for his own wrong decisions and errors. His friends began to shun him and his health was adversely affected by his gloom and despondency. He refused counseling and went on welfare.

Here you have two brothers who experienced the same loss. One reacted constructively and the other reacted negatively and with a complete sense of futility. It is not what happens to us individually that matters so much; it is our thought about it, our reaction, which can be constructive or negative. One brother used his imagination wisely, rebuilding in his mind a new pattern, seeing future possibilities, using the wings of faith and imagination for rebuilding a better life. He discovered that success and wealth were in his own mind.

Replace Negative Thoughts with Positive Thoughts

When you cohabit with negative thoughts, your Life Force gets snarled up in your subconscious mind just as when you put your foot on a garden hose and block the flow of water. The negative emotions that are dammed up in your subconscious then come forth as all manner of diseases, both mental and physical.

Cast out negativism, ill will, criticism, and self-condemnation, and instead fill your mind with constructive thoughts of harmony, health, peace, joy, and goodwill, and you will transform your life.

By thinking constructively, based on universal principles, you can change all the negative patterns in your mind and thereafter live a charmed life.

To walk the royal road to riches of all kinds—spiritual, mental, material, and financial—you must never place obstacles and impediments in the pathway of others; neither must you be jealous, envious, or resentful of others. Remember, your thoughts are creative and whatever you think about another you are creating in your own life and experience.

In many work environments, employees compete with each other for advancement and increased power. Some people are so competitive that they will go to extremes to sabotage rivals for the promotion they seek.

Barry G.'s performance over the years had been superior. He had been praised for his innovations and complimented on the quality of his work. His boss was to retire at the end of the year and Barry expected to be promoted to his job. However, six months ago, Carl R. was transferred into the department. He had been passed over for promotion in his previous assignment and now began a campaign to obtain the promotion in this department.

He identified Barry as his chief rival for the promotion and looked for ways to demean him and build up his own chances. At meetings he'd pooh-pooh Barry's suggestions. He'd go out of his way to get the boss's attention for his activities and, whenever possible, he'd make Barry's work more difficult.

Barry seethed with resentment. He had worked hard for years to obtain the promotion and now Carl was pushing him out. After much thought, and discussion with close friends and his pastor, Barry realized that he could not beat a schemer like Carl at his own game. He chose a different path.

He would concentrate on his own assets and not on Carl's ploys. He meditated: "Carl is a competent worker. His ambition is logical and he has many assets that are valuable to our department. I am at least equal to him and have proven myself over and over again. I will continue to concentrate on my work and on achieving my goal. Nothing Carl can do or say can influence the way I work or think about myself."

As a result, Barry's work continued to be superior, and when the boss retired, Barry received the promotion.

A negative thought or suggestion by another person has no power unless you give it power. Suggestions are *a* power, but they are not *the* Power that moves as harmony, beauty, love, and peace. When those around you are expressing negativity or are casting negative suggestions toward you, always remember that you have the ability to unite mentally with the Infinite Intelligence within you, whose principles are love, generosity, and harmony—not negativity.

Never finish a negative statement; reverse it immediately and wonders will happen in your life. If you have indulged in fear, worry, and other destructive forms of thinking, your subconscious mind will have accepted your negative thoughts as requests and will proceed to bring them into your experience. The remedy is to begin devoting your thoughts to kindness, peace, and forgiveness. Your subconscious mind, being creative, will then equally proceed to create the attributes in your life that you have earnestly decreed.

Every time you think or say negative thoughts, you help prolong the situation that is wrecking your peace of mind and ensuring failure in your endeavor. In effect, you are praying against yourself. Make your inner, silent thought conform to your desired aim. Failure is negative thinking. It has many causes. One of them, perhaps the most crucial, is the conviction that failure is inevitable.

Every part of your being then expresses these thoughts; your outer life will demonstrate what you are consciously impressing in your subconscious mind. Never affirm inwardly, therefore, anything you do not want to experience outwardly.

Ambition Is Essential

Many people would do fairly well in life if they only had somebody to keep stirring them up all the time, recharging them, enthusing them, constantly inspiring them; but they have no inclination to do this for themselves and hence remain in mediocrity. They depend on others for their motor power. When you give them a good talking-to, raise their hopes, and fire their ambition by telling them what is possible for them, you recharge them as one would an automobile battery. They run splendidly for a few days, and you think they are going to turn over a new leaf and keep their enthusiasm up, but all at once they collapse. Their power is gone, and they have to be recharged.

They seem absolutely incapable of self-locomotion. They lack initiative, self-direction. They have to be pushed about like the pieces on a checkerboard. When conscious of standing alone, with no one to lean on or to supply motor power, they are dazed; they do not seem to know what to do.

There are plenty of men and women who seem very ambitious to get on, but they lack self-propelling power. They wait for something to happen, for somebody to push them into a position, an influential friend to advance them.

These people slide along the line of least resistance. They would very much like success, but are afraid of the price. The successful life is too strenuous for them. There are too many difficulties in it, it requires too much sticking to it and hanging on in face of seemingly insurmountable obstacles. These people go about with an indefinite idea that there is something in the world for them somewhere, and that by some chance it will come to them if they only wait long enough. In the meantime, they are content to be propped up and supported by others. This lack of self-reliance, this dependence on outside power, is fatal to all advancement and achievement.

Sam L. was frustrated. He told his career counselor that he'd never expected to have to look for a job. "I always thought my father or my uncle would hire me in their businesses. Even after their business failed, I assumed that with all of the contacts my family had, I'd be hired by one of them."

Sam had never considered doing something for himself. All of his life, things were done for him. But despite his good education, for the first time he had nobody to depend on but himself.

Sam had to face up to the real world. By working closely with his counselor over several weeks, he was able to evaluate his strengths and weaknesses, the areas in which he was happy and those he disliked, the job opportunities in a variety of areas, any additional training he needed to obtain the kind of job he would like, and most of all to train his mind to accept that he must be self-reliant, that he could not rely on anyone but himself if he was to become a truly well-integrated human being.

You don't, as a rule, rise by accident from the slums and obscurity to wealth, honor, and fame by saving someone from drowning at the seashore or by meeting a millionaire who likes you. Remember a simple truth: You will always demonstrate your character, your state of mind. Character is destiny. Character is the way you think, feel, and believe, the spiritual values you have enthroned in your mind, the integrity and honesty that you have established there. These qualities pay dividends.

Techniques for Overcoming Negative Thinking

The ideal way to rid yourself of unwanted emotions is to practice the law of substitution. *Substitute a positive, constructive thought for the negative thought.* When negative thoughts enter your mind, do not fight them; instead, just say to yourself: "My faith is in all things good." You will find the negative thoughts disappear just as light dispels the darkness.

At times you will find your mind falling back into its old habits of fretting, fussing, worrying, and recounting the verdicts of others. When these thoughts come to your mind, issue the order "Stop! My thoughts are the way I feed my subconscious." Whether it be a job-related or a personal matter, do this a hundred times a day, or a thousand times, if necessary.

Many people when faced with a catastrophe lose hope and become negative about everything. But with others a catastrophe leads to strength and heroic motivation even under the most dreaded of conditions. Susan and Sherman Goldstein's Martha's Vineyard (Massachusetts) inn was destroyed by fire in December of 2001. They were so challenged that they didn't have time to make dinner for a month and had to be fed by friends and given living space by another business owner.

They did not let this disaster dominate their lives. They chose to reopen the inn's restaurant first, to maintain a presence in the town, and during restorations they wrapped their destroyed inn with a giant banner, reading, "When life gives you lemons, make lemonade." The Goldsteins used the fire as an opportunity to transform a very modest inn, whose rooms were old and small, into a top-shelf facility renamed Mansion House, catering to a larger clientele. Susan Goldstein says the fire that destroyed so much actually helped them to reach a new level. Their positive thinking enabled them to rebuild and start afresh.

Visualization

Visualize just how you will deal with the challenges you face each day. If you are going to make a sales presentation or prepare a report for a management meeting or engage in any productive activity, plan out in your mind just what you will say, how you will say it, what steps you will take to achieve it. Rehearse it over and over again in your mind. It will enter deep into your subconscious; it will permeate every cell of your brain. You will become committed to success and when you actually are selling to that customer, standing before that management group, or engaging in the activity, your subconscious will take over and you will achieve the desired results.

Thank Goodness It's Monday

The expression TGIF, "Thank goodness it's Friday," is now accepted as the typical attitude of most American workers. We look forward to our weekend and its respite from our jobs and careers. There is nothing wrong with this, as we all should rejoice in our days of rest. However, ambitious and successful people look forward just as much to resuming their work on Monday.

Many people talk about "blue Monday." These people are already resigning themselves to their "fate" and beginning to shut down their lives. Monday then comes with a certain sense of resignation: On Sunday they were consciously decreeing their future, and their subconscious responded accordingly. In all probability, they didn't even know that they had planned ahead and had thus created their "fate." If you replace this resignation with positive thoughts about the work you are doing and anticipation of its challenges and opportunities, you will eradicate those Monday morning blues.

SUM AND SUBSTANCE

- Positive thinking starts with understanding the power of the subconscious.

- Take control of your career. Don't let your boss, your coworkers, or anyone else steer your "career-ship." Never forget that you have the internal power to overcome negative influences that could stymie your career growth.

- There is nothing else so helpful as the carrying of an optimistic, expectant attitude—the attitude which always looks for the best, the highest, the happiest—and never allowing oneself to get into a pessimistic, discouraged mood.

- Never finish a negative statement; reverse it immediately and wonders will happen in your life. Your subconscious mind, being creative, will then equally proceed to create the attributes in your life that you have earnestly decreed.

- Visualize just how you will deal with the challenges you face each day. If you are going to make a sales presentation or prepare a report for a management meeting or engage in any productive activity, plan out in your mind just what you will say, how you will say it, what steps you will take.

Chapter Four

Mastering the Law of Attraction

Men and women are human magnets. Just as a steel magnet drawn through a pile of rubbish will pull out only the things that have an affinity for it, so we are constantly drawing to us, and establishing relations with, the things and the people that respond to our thoughts and ideals.

Why do some people win the attention of others easily, are able to make friends readily and gain the admiration of others, while others just barely get along?

When we meet some people, we are impressed by their pleasant "personality." Something about the way they project themselves makes us feel confident in them, admire them, and feel comfortable with them. These people have mastered the law of attraction. They attract the attention of their bosses, their customers, and others. Such men and women are the people we choose to be our mentors. It is from this group that the leaders of companies are chosen, and it is these people who climb readily up the ladder of success.

The American psychologist William James defined personality as a set of individually evolved characteristic patterns of behavior, which determines daily functioning on both conscious and unconscious levels. Personality is said to represent the balance between innate drives and a combination of conscious and external controls.

The important thing to remember is that attractive characteristics can be *developed*. Some facets of us are inborn—our physical appearance, basic intelligence, and some talents—but each of us has the capacity to make the most of our innate traits and to develop them to give us that type of personality that others will admire. We can learn how to use the law of attraction.

It's not easy to grow into the person you want to be, but it starts with a strong desire and commitment to develop your innate traits. You can develop an outgoing, cheerful, optimistic, and positive demeanor—a personality that will win the approbation of the men and women with whom you interrelate.

Personality Traits Can Be Acquired

William James commented that your personality is the sum total of all of your traits. This includes your body and your psychic powers, but also your clothes, your house, your spouse and children, your ancestors and friends, your reputation and works, your possessions, and your bank account. All these things generate the same range of emotions. If they wax and prosper, you feel triumphant; if they dwindle and die away, you feel cast down—not necessarily in the same degree for each thing, but in much the same way for all.

Our personality is the way in which we express ourselves to the outside world. We are not only gregarious animals, liking to be in the sight of our fellows, but we have an innate propensity to get ourselves noticed, and noticed favorably, by our kind.

Certain personalities are greater than mere physical beauty and more powerful than learning. Charm of personality is a divine gift that sways the strongest characters, leads to high-level career positions, and sometimes even controls the destinies of nations.

People who possess this magnetic power unconsciously influence us. The moment we come into their presence we have a sense of enlargement. They inspire their subordinates on the job, their customers or clients, and others look to them as models in their own careers and lives. They unlock within us possibilities of which we previously had no conception. Our horizon broadens; we feel a new power stirring through all our being; we experience a sense of relief, as if a great weight had been removed that long had pressed upon us.

Much of the charm of a magnetic personality comes from a fine, cultivated manner. Tact, also, is a very important element—perhaps the most important. One must know exactly what to do, and be able to do just the right thing at the proper time. Good judgment and common sense are indispensable to those who are trying to acquire this magic power. Good taste is also one of the elements of personal charm. You cannot offend the tastes of others without hurting their sensibilities.

One of the greatest investments one can make is that of attaining a gracious manner, cordiality of bearing, and generosity of feeling—the delightful art of pleasing. It is infinitely better than money capital, for all doors fly open to sunny, pleasing personalities. They are more than welcome; they are sought for everywhere.

Personality traits can be acquired. Granting that all people have equal rights and opportunities, we must recognize that all do not have equal intelligence, equal physical strength, or equal levels of energy; yet whatever their status, they may rise by self-education and self-development. Those eager for knowledge and ambitious to excel will naturally forge ahead. You can choose and work to develop the personality traits you wish to acquire. Application is the great thing.

The principal qualities that make the stature of the perfect human being are patience, kindness, generosity, humility, courtesy, unselfishness, good temper, and sincerity. These traits are not in-born; they can be developed. Take these as the framework of the personality you wish to create out of the qualities found in your own complex nature.

Unfortunately, some people who have all these qualities are not perceived to have a pleasant personality because they lack a good appearance. This doesn't mean physical beauty. You need not be born with a beautiful face or physique to project a good appearance, but unless you dress neatly and appropriately, wear a smile instead of a frown, and are clean and well groomed, your high qualities will not be noticed.

Appearance is important since it is the first impression others have of you that often determines whether they will give you an opportunity to demonstrate your superior qualities.

Not only are you judged by how you appear, but also you judge others by their appearance. Instinctively, people attempt to cultivate in themselves the positive qualities of appearance they see in those they admire. They wear the same type of clothes, imitate their hairstyles, and act in the same manner as their models. You can do this with other qualities as well. Concentrate on the personality characteristics of people you respect and look up to. In this person you can visualize the person you wish to be. Look not only at men and women whom you know, but also take models from the past and present of others who are exemplars of the ideal personality you wish to have.

Look for the Good

It is just as easy to go through life looking for the good and the beautiful instead of the ugly; for the noble instead of the ignoble; for the bright and cheerful instead of the dark and gloomy; the hopeful instead of the despairing; to see the bright side instead of the dark side. To set your face always toward the sunlight is just as easy as to see always the shadows, and it makes all the difference in your character between content and discontent, between happiness and misery, and in your life between prosperity and adversity, between success and failure. Feed these thoughts into your subconscious mind. This is how to apply the law of attraction.

Learn to look for the light, then. Positively refuse to harbor shadows and blots, negative images, the discordant. Hold to those things that give pleasure, that are helpful and inspiring, and you will change your whole way of looking at things, will transform your personality in a very short time.

One way to develop the best traits in yourself is to look for the best traits in others. By taking a largehearted attitude toward everyone you meet, by trying to pierce through the mask of the outer man or woman, to the innermost core, and by cultivating kindly feelings toward all, you can acquire this inestimable gift.

Nothing will pay you better than acquiring the power to make others feel at ease, happy, and satisfied with themselves. Sunny people dispel melancholy, gloom, worry, and anxiety from all those with whom they come in contact, just as the sun drives away darkness. When they enter a roomful of people, where the conversation has been lagging, and where everybody seems bored, they transform the surroundings like the sun bursting through thick, black clouds after a storm. Everybody takes on a joyous spirit from the glad soul who just entered; tongues are untied, conversation which dragged becomes bright and spirited, and the whole atmosphere vibrates with gladness and good cheer.

Be empathetic. Empathetic people put themselves in the shoes of the person with whom they interrelate. They not only hear what that person says, but they feel what he or she feels at that moment. How can anyone fail to respond positively to such people?

Maintain a Cheerful Disposition
Unless you have a mental attitude that is free of bitterness and guile and you look at each day as a blessing to be enjoyed and savored, you will have an unhappy and most likely unproductive life.

We cannot do our best work while we harbor revengeful or even unfriendly thoughts toward others. Our faculties only give up their best when working in perfect harmony. There must be goodwill in the heart or we cannot do good work with head or hand. Hatred, revenge, and jealousy are poisons, as fatal to all that is noblest in us as arsenic is fatal to physical life.

A kindly attitude, a feeling of goodwill toward others, is our best protection against bitter hatred or injurious thoughts of any kind.

In a gracious personality there is a charm from which it is very hard to get away. It is difficult to snub the person who possesses it. There is something about him or her that attracts you. No matter how busy or how worried you may be, or how much you may dislike to be interrupted, somehow you haven't the heart to turn away a person with a pleasing personality.

The Secret of Being Pleasant

Emerson says, "What you are speaks so loudly that I cannot hear what you say." We cannot conceal what we are, how we feel, because we radiate our atmosphere, our personality; and this is cold or warm, attractive or repellent, according to our dominant traits and qualities.

A person who is selfish, always thinking of him- or herself and looking out for his or her own advantage, who is cold, unsympathetic, greedy, cannot radiate a warm, mellow atmosphere. If selfishness, indifference, avarice, and greed are dominant in your nature, you will radiate it and it will repel others because these are the qualities people instinctively detest.

The qualities that attract are outflowing, buoyant; the qualities that repel are inflowing. That is, people who have no magnetism are self-centered; they think too much about themselves. They do not give out enough; they are always after something, absorbing, receiving some benefit, trying to get some advantage for themselves. They lack sympathy, lack cordiality, good fellowship; they are bad mixers.

A piece of magnetized steel will attract only the products of iron ore. It has no affinity for wood, copper, rubber, or any other substance that has no iron in it. When you were a child you found that your little steel magnet would pick up a needle but not a match or a toothpick. It would draw to itself only that like itself.

Men and women are human magnets. Just as a steel magnet drawn through a pile of rubbish will pull out only the things that have an affinity for it, so we are constantly drawing to us, establishing relations with, the things and the people that respond to our thoughts and ideals.

Our environment, our associates, our general condition are the result of our mental attraction. These things have come to us on the physical plane because we have concentrated on them, have related ourselves to them mentally; they are our affinities, and will remain with us as long as the affinity for them continues to exist in our minds.

Applying the Law of Attraction

Some people are naturally magnetic, but when you analyze their character you will find they possess certain qualities that we all instinctively admire, the qualities that attract every single human being, such as generosity, magnanimity, cordiality, broad sympathies, large views of life, helpfulness, optimism. They are followers of the law of attraction.

There is not one of these qualities that you cannot cultivate and strengthen a great deal. If you do so, you will get a hearing where others will not.

Whatever your business, your reputation and your success will depend in a great degree on the quality of the impression you make upon others. It means everything, therefore, to young men and women to use the law of attraction to develop a magnetic, forceful, attractive personality. Cultivate the heart qualities. Intellect and brainpower have little, if anything, to do with personal magnetism. It is the lovable, not the intellectual, that draws and holds people.

This is not a very difficult thing to do. Everyone can cultivate the ability to please and the strength of character that will make him or her felt as a real force in the world. Knowing the law of attraction—the qualities and characteristics that distinguish the magnetic and nonmagnetic—it is comparatively easy to cultivate the one and to eliminate the other. That is, we can cultivate the generous, magnanimous, cheerful, helpful mental qualities and crush their opposites; and in proportion as we do this we shall find ourselves becoming more interested in others, and they in turn becoming more interested in us. As we make ourselves personal magnets by fashioning our aura of the kindly thoughts and words and deeds that day by day go to the making of a rich, magnetic personality, we shall find ourselves more welcome wherever we go, more sought after; we shall attract people to us more and more.

By imbuing your subconscious mind with the qualities that you admire so much in others—the very qualities that attract you—you will become attractive to others. As you become permeated with these qualities, they shall characterize you, and you will acquire a magnetic, attractive personality.

Live a Healthy Life

The first step toward making yourself magnetic is to build up your health. Vigorous health, coupled with a right mental attitude, an optimistic, hopeful, cheerful, happy mind, will increase your magnetism wonderfully.

A person with robust health radiates an atmosphere of strength, vigor, and courage, while one who lacks vitality drains from others instead of giving to them. Physical force and abounding joyousness of health help to create a magnetic, forceful personality. People with buoyant, alert minds, with a sparkle in their eyes and elasticity in their step, and who are bubbling over with abundant physical vitality, have a tremendous advantage over those who are devitalized and physically weak.

Admit Your Mistakes

One way to turn people off is to be a bumptious, self-important, arrogant individual who never admits a mistake.

Investment guru Warren Buffett, probably one of the richest people in the world, not only knows how to use "failure" and "mistakes," but he goes so far as to advertise them. In 1989 he started a formal practice of telling on himself by publishing a list of his mistakes in his "Letter to Investors." In this letter, Buffett confessed not only mistakes made, but opportunities lost because he failed to act appropriately. It is Buffett's belief that candor benefits the manager at least as much as the shareholder. He puts it this way: "The CEO who misleads others in public may eventually mislead himself in private." Buffett believes in the value of studying one's mistakes, rather than concentrating only on success.

Perhaps it's this level of candor that frees Warren Buffett to be joyful at work. He is known for always being upbeat and supportive, genuinely excited about coming to work every day. People are attracted to him. Is it because he is rich? Or is it the other way around?

Reach Out to Those You Meet

You must make people feel that they have met a sincere person. Don't greet people with a stiff "How do you do?" or "Glad to meet you," without any feeling, any sentiment in it. Be a good mixer. Look people you meet squarely in the eye and make them feel your personality. Give them a glad hand, with a smile and kind word to make them remember that they have come in contact with a real force, and make them glad to meet you again.

If you are to be popular, you must cultivate cordiality. You must fling the door of your heart wide open and not, as many do, just leave it slightly ajar, as much as to say to people you meet, "You may peep in a bit, but you cannot come in until I know whether you will be a desirable acquaintance." A great many people are stingy with their cordiality. They seem to reserve it for some special occasion or for intimate friends. They think it is too precious to give out to everybody.

You will be surprised to see what this warm, glad handshake and cordial greeting will do in creating a bond of goodwill between you and everybody you meet. People who meet you will say to themselves, "Well, there is a really interesting personality. I want to know more about this lady or gentleman. This is an unusual greeting. This person sees something in me, evidently, which most people do not see."

Cultivate the habit of being cordial, of meeting people with a warm, sincere greeting, with an open heart; it will do wonders for you. You will find that the stiffness, diffidence, and indifference, the cold lack of interest in everybody that now so troubles you, will disappear. People will see that you really take an interest in them, that you really want to know, please, and interest them. The practice of cordiality will revolutionize your social power. You will develop attractive qualities that you never before dreamed you possessed. Others will flock to you, look to you for guidance, and help you realize your dreams.

Choose a Mentor—Be a Mentor

An excellent way to move ahead in your career is to seek and follow a mentor. This man or woman has all of the attributes discussed above and is not only able but also willing to share them with others.

Mentors are good exemplars of people who have mastered the law of attraction. They can not only provide you with knowledge, but also guide you through the nuances of company culture.

And, when you have achieved success and have moved into a leadership position, you can repay your mentor by becoming a mentor to a newcomer to the organization.

SUM AND SUBSTANCE

- Unless you have a mental attitude that is free of bitterness and guile and you look at each day as a blessing to be enjoyed and savored, you will have an unhappy and most likely unproductive life. Banish negativity from your thoughts.

- Know the law of attraction—the qualities and characteristics that distinguish the magnetic and the nonmagnetic. We can cultivate the generous, magnanimous, cheerful, helpful mental qualities and crush their opposites; and as we do this we shall find ourselves becoming more interested in others, and they in turn becoming more interested in us.

- Study the men and women—those you know personally and those from the past and present times about whom you have read—whose personalities you admire. Use them as models for your behavior.

- Learn to radiate joy and generosity. Fling out your gladness without reserve.

- Be empathetic. Empathetic people put themselves in the shoes of the people with whom they interrelate. They not only hear what others say, but feel what they feel when they say it. People cannot help but respond positively to such people.

- Be enthusiastic. People who are enthusiastic about themselves and whose actions undertake their work with the assurance of success will realize the fulfillment of their promise. Enthusiasm multiplies your power, raises whatever ability you have to its highest level.

- One way to implement the law of attraction in the workplace is to encourage your associates to express their ideas, especially when they differ from yours. This not only provides you with new ideas, but also makes them realize that you recognize their talents and look upon them as partners not subordinates.

- Seek and then follow a mentor, a person you admire and from whom you can learn. When you have achieved success, offer your services as a mentor to others.

Chapter Five

Becoming a More Enthusiastic Person

Enthusiasm is the secret ingredient of success for the most successful people as well as the generator of happiness in the lives of those who possess it.

The word "enthusiasm" comes from the Greek, and literally means to be possessed by God. It means an absorbing or controlling possession of the mind by any interest or pursuit. You must believe that the energy of the Infinite Power animates you and the creative ideas that unfold within you reveal everything you need to know. You must have faith in the response of the Infinite Power to help you attain your goal. This generates enthusiasm, which is awakened by your positive faith. Gradually a new world of achievement opens up for you.

People with pleasing personalities are enthusiastic about their lives, their work, their relationships, and their goals. Enthusiasm comes from deep within ourselves. Enthusiasm cannot be faked. Feigned enthusiasm through artificial gestures, phony smiles, and exaggerated comments is easily detected. If you believe that what you are doing is worthwhile, meaningful, exciting, and achievable, it will show up in your demeanor and your actions.

Be Enthusiastic About Your Work

Why is it that one employee can often accomplish three or four times as much as another employee? The difference is not always that of ability. It is often a difference in the character of the effort. Successful people try harder. They add enthusiasm and a splendid zest to their work that increases the quality as well as the quantity of the result.

I have often heard employees say in the morning that they fairly dreaded the day's work, that the hours dragged and that they were glad when the ordeal was over. They felt no enthusiasm for their employment. Should anyone hope to succeed in life who considers a day's work an ordeal, who goes to it as a slave lashed to his task?

It is the employees who take hold of their work as though they love it, who take pride in it, who are made of the winning material. There is nothing that troubles an employer more than to see employees doing things in an ambitionless, indifferent manner, as though they regard their work as a necessary evil to be done to keep them from starving.

Employees who go to their tasks with energy, determination, and enthusiasm give confidence to the employer that the thing they undertake will not only be done, but be well done.

When employees drag themselves about as though existence were a burden, when they take hold of the work with repugnance or dread, the employer knows that they will never amount to anything.

Enthusiasm Is Contagious

The world has always made way for enthusiasm. It multiplies your power, raises whatever ability you have to its highest level.

Enthusiasm attracts business. It is so contagious that before we know it, we are infected with it, even if we try to brace ourselves against it. If your heart is in your work, your enthusiasm will often cause a would-be customer to forget that you are trying to make a sale.

There are people who do splendid work when their enthusiasm is up. When they are enthusiastic, they are productive, prolific in ideas, original, creative, strong, and effective; but let their enthusiasm cool a bit, and they are all down at the heel. All their standards drop and they are good for nothing during the ebb tide. They just have to wait for flood tide. You meet them one day, and you would think they were going to do marvels, and perhaps the very next day they are low-spirited and pessimistic; their work drags, and they are shorn of their power until they get a fresh supply of energy.

Krista Hawkin is a woman who never loses her enthusiasm. She fires up hundreds of potential customers every week, and is famous for it. She's not a manager, a sales executive, or a leader in the usual sense. She gives tours of a Hyundai Motors manufacturing facility in Montgomery, Alabama, one of the most technically advanced facilities in the world, turning out a thousand cars a day.

Krista is well known for turning tourists into customers with her passion and enthusiasm. She takes a personal interest in the men and women on her tour, encourages them to ask questions, and answers them fully, enthusiastically, and in nontechnical terms.

Experts know that everyone who works for a brand represents it to the outside world, and every interaction is an opportunity to put an energized, enthusiastic face to the brand. Krista means it, which is why she's effective. She says she sees what the plant has done for the community and the state of Alabama, which makes it easy for her to be happy. She never uses the term "employees." To her, everyone is a team member, and the quality of the vehicles is directly related to the energy of the people making them. She does not start a tour with the purpose of selling cars; her goal is to entertain and inform visitors, and it has paid off in increased sales.

Maintain Your Enthusiasm

Enthusiasm is fragile. It can easily be lost. It is a great art to learn how to keep up your enthusiasm amid discouragement, but it is one you can easily acquire. It is simply a question of controlling thought. We can keep the negative thoughts out of our minds. There is nothing that will dampen the enthusiasm and take the edge off of an endeavor more quickly than to flood the mind with destructive, discordant thoughts. We can control the mood, and the best way to keep out the darkness is to flood the mind with sunlight.

One way to generate enthusiasm is to assume the part you wish to play and then play it with enthusiasm. If you are ambitious to do big things, you must always be enthusiastic about yourself.

Tom J. knew it would be a tough job to persuade his manager to upgrade their computer system. To overcome his boss's concern about the added cost, he prepared an exciting presentation on how the proposed system would speed up the work and minimize errors. He knew his boss was usually reluctant to accept ideas, and his first thought was "Why bother? He won't do anything anyway." But Tom was so enthusiastic about the project, he overcame his reluctance and made an exciting and spirited presentation, and won his boss's support for the new system.

There is something in the atmosphere of enthusiastic people who believe they are going to win, something in their very appearance that wins half the battle before a blow is struck.

Set your mind toward the thing you want to accomplish, so resolutely, so definitely, and with such enthusiastic determination, and put so much grit into your resolution, that nothing on earth can turn you from your purpose until you attain it.

Lucy A. was seeking her first job as an administrative assistant in the medical field. She had an associate's degree in medical administration from a community college, but was turned down several times because of lack of work experience. So she gave herself a pep talk: "I want this job. I have the technical know-how. I am a diligent and conscientious worker. I can be a real asset to the doctor." When she went for her next interview, she was determined to get the job. She repeated her pep talk over and over again on the way to the doctor's office. She entered the office confidently, and answered the doctor's questions with such enthusiasm that he offered her a job. Some months later he told her that when he saw from her application that she had no experience, he had decided to just give her a courtesy interview and reject her, but her enthusiasm convinced him to try her in the job. She carried that enthusiasm into the work itself and became a valuable member of his administrative staff.

Are You a Lifter or a Leaner?

There are two kinds of people—just two kinds of people—no more. Not the good and the bad, for it is well understood the good are half-bad and the bad are half-good. Not the happy and the sad, not the rich and the poor, not the humble and the proud. No. *The two kinds of people on earth are the people who lift and the people who lean.* Wherever you go, you will find the world's masses are ever divided into just these two classes. And, strangely enough, you will find, too, it seems that there is only one lifter for twenty who lean. Are you a lifter? Are you a leaner or whiner? Do you lean on others? You are here to grow, to transcend. You are here to meet problems, difficulties, and challenges and to overcome them. You are not here to run away from them. The joy is in overcoming. If the crossword puzzle were filled out for you, it would be very insipid. The joy is in solving the puzzle.

The engineer rejoices in overcoming all obstacles, failures, and difficulties in building a bridge. You are here to sharpen your mental and spiritual tools while you grow in wisdom, strength, and understanding. You are here to build enthusiasm in your life and the lives of those with whom you relate.

Enthusiasm Leads to Achievement

When we are enthusiastic about something we are doing, the excitement, the joy, the inner feeling of satisfaction permeates the entire activity. It is not always easy to be excited about many of the things we have to do on a day-by-day basis, but it is possible if we only make the effort.

What goes on in the mind is what determines outcome. When you really get enthusiastic, you can see it in the flash of your eyes, in your alert and vibrant personality. You can see it in the spring of your step. You can see it in the verve of your whole being. Enthusiasm makes the difference in your attitude toward other people, toward your job, toward the world. It makes the big difference in the zest and delight of human existence.

You must, of course, be enthusiastic about yourself and your abilities, but it is also necessary to be enthusiastic about what you are doing—the product you are making or selling, the music you are composing, or the essay you are writing.

How can you become enthusiastic about something? You must first believe in what you are doing. Learn as much about the product, the idea, or the concept that you are engaged in. Get as much information as you can. Delve into your subject. Live it. The more you learn, the more you make your subject part of your life, and your enthusiasm for it will grow.

When we study the lives of great men and women, whether they are in the field of government, business, science, or the arts, we see that the one common ingredient all of them possess is enthusiasm about their work and their lives. Enthusiasm enabled Beethoven to compose his greatest symphonies despite his deafness. Enthusiasm enabled Columbus to persuade Queen Isabella to finance his voyage of discovery and to keep going when it seemed impossible to succeed.

You, too, have this power. Release your talents and abilities and develop a zeal and enthusiasm to learn more about your inner powers. You then can lift yourself up to astonishing heights. Ask the Supreme Intelligence within you to give you what you need and it will respond to you. Realize Infinite Intelligence is guiding you, revealing hidden talents to you, opening up new doors for you, showing you the way you should go; and the Guiding Principle within you will lead and guide you in all your ways.

SUM AND SUBSTANCE

- Set your mind toward the thing you would like to accomplish, so resolutely, so definitely, and with such enthusiastic determination that nothing on earth can turn you from your purpose until you attain it.

- Successful people try harder. They add enthusiasm and a splendid zest to their work, which increases the quality as well as the quantity of the result.

- When we are enthusiastic about something we are doing, the excitement, the joy, the inner feeling of satisfaction permeates the entire activity. It is not always easy to be excited about many of the things we have to do on a day-by-day basis, but it is possible if we only make the effort.

- Enthusiasm is contagious. When you are enthusiastic, your eyes sparkle, your voice vibrates, your step becomes springier. It permeates every aspect of your demeanor and personality. Your boss sees it; your subordinates and coworkers feel it; your customers are influenced by it.

- Enthusiasm is fragile. It can easily be lost. It is a great art to learn how to keep up your enthusiasm amid discouragement, but it is one you can easily acquire. It is simply a question of controlling thought. We can keep the negative thoughts out of our minds. There is nothing that will dampen enthusiasm and take the edge off of endeavors more quickly than to flood the mind with destructive, discordant thoughts. We can control the mood, and the best way to keep out the darkness is to flood the mind with sunlight.

Chapter Six

Developing Resilience and Adaptability

Our subconscious convictions and conditioning dictate and control all of our conscious actions. You can recondition your mind by identifying yourself with the eternal verities. You can develop a marvelous and wonderful personality by filling your mind with the concepts of peace, joy, love, good humor, happiness, and goodwill. Busy your mind with these ideas. As you do, they will sink into the subconscious level.

You've heard that old saying "If it ain't broke, don't fix it." There's some truth in it, as changing things just for the sake of change is unproductive. However, in order to move ahead, to tackle new challenges, change is often necessary. It's easy to just keep doing the same thing over and over again. It's even more tempting to resist change when what you are doing was developed by you. We often fall in love with our own ideas and are reluctant to consider changes—even when they would lead to improvement.

Another reason many people refuse to consider change is fear of failure. Nobody wants to suffer the pains of defeat, but no endeavor can succeed unless it is attempted, and with every attempt there is the risk that it may not work.

To ensure that you are willing to review and reassess everything you do in order to make necessary changes, you must condition your subconscious mind to be adaptable. If you continuously re-inforce open-mindedness and flexibility, your subconscious mind, instead of resisting changes to the status quo, will become a vehicle for adapting new concepts. Successful people take risks. They do not limit themselves to approaches that they have always used.

Sure, you may fail, but you must develop resilience so you can accept failures and bounce back. We must learn from our mistakes and apply what we learn to overcome our failures. R. H. Macy had to close his first seven Macy's stores, but instead of giving up as a "failure," he kept trying and became one of America's leading re-tailers. Babe Ruth struck out more than 1300 times in his career, but that is forgotten because of his 714 home runs. Thomas Edison never gave up, but perseverance alone is not enough. Each time one of his experiments failed, he studied what caused the failure and kept seeking solutions. His resilience and adaptability was honed by his failures. They did not defeat him, but motivated him to keep trying.

Only You Can Change You

If you are rigid in your thinking and not adaptable, you must overcome that rigidity. Nobody can do it for you. The first thing you must accept is that you are the only one who can change yourself. This is the beginning of a real change in your entire per-sonality.

Mentally divide yourself into two people: your present self and that which you desire to be. Look at the thoughts of fear, worry, anxiety, jealousy, or hatred that may be enslaving and imprisoning you. You have divided yourself into two for the purpose of disci-plining yourself. One part of you is the human mind working in you; the other is the Infinite seeking expression through you. It all depends on how you see yourself.

In an Asian country, there is a legend about a farmer who went to a wise man in his village and told him about his life and how things were so hard. He did not know how he was going to make it. Fear of the future dominated his mind. He wanted to give up; he was tired of fighting and struggling. It seemed that as one problem was solved, a new one arose.

The wise man asked him to go down to the lake and bring back a bucket of water. He then poured the water into three pots and placed each on a hook over the fireplace. Soon the pots came to boil. In the first he placed a bunch of carrots, in the second he placed a few eggs, and in the last he placed a handful of tea leaves.

After they'd boiled for half an hour, he removed the pots from the fireplace. He took the carrots out and put them in a bowl; he then took the eggs out and put them in another bowl; and lastly he poured the tea into a third bowl. Turning to the farmer, he asked, "Tell me, what do you see?"

"Carrots, eggs, and tea," the farmer replied. Then the wise man said: "Pick up the carrots and tell me what you feel." The farmer did so and said, "The carrots are soft." Then the wise man ordered the farmer to take an egg and break it. After pulling off the shell, the farmer observed that the egg had become hard. Finally, the wise man asked the farmer to sip the tea. The farmer smiled as he tasted its rich flavor. The farmer then asked, "What does this mean?"

The wise man explained that each of these objects had faced the same adversity . . . boiling water. Each reacted differently. The carrot went in strong and hard. However, subjected to the boiling water, it softened and became weak. The egg had been fragile. Its thin outer shell had protected its soft interior, but the boiling water hardened its inside. The tea leaves were unique, however. They had changed the water.

"Which are you?" he asked the farmer. "When adversity knocks on your door, how do you respond? Are you a carrot, an egg, or a tea leaf?"

As you look at the problems you face in your life, ask yourself:

"Which am I? Am I the carrot that seems strong, but with pain and adversity do I become soft and lose my strength? Am I the egg that starts with a fragile heart and a fluid spirit, but after the loss of a job, a breakup, a financial hardship, or some other trial, have I become hardened and stiff? Or am I like the tea leaf? The leaf actually changes the hot water—the very circumstance that brings the pain. When the water gets hot, it releases fragrance and flavor. If you are like the tea leaf, when things are at their worst, you get better and change the situation around you. When the hour is the darkest and trials are the greatest, do you elevate yourself to another level?

How do you handle adversity? Are you a carrot, an egg, or a tea leaf?

Positive Thinking Encourages Adaptability

Remember this great truth: You do not have to go along with familiar practices or systems or react mechanically as you formerly did. React and think in a new way. You want to be an achiever. Therefore, from this moment forward, you must refuse to identify with the negative thoughts that tend to drag you down, and adapt your thinking to solving the problems you face in a new and different way.

Be Persistent

The story of one of America's greatest statesmen is not a story of easy success but one of dogged persistence. He failed in business at twenty-one and was defeated for the state legislature in 1833. He was elected in 1834. His sweetheart died in 1835. He had a nervous breakdown in 1836. He was defeated for speaker in 1838. He was defeated for elector in 1840. He was defeated for Congress in 1843. Finally, he was elected for one term in Congress in 1846, only to be defeated again for Congress in 1848. He was defeated for the Senate in 1855, was defeated for vice president in 1856, and was defeated again for the Senate in 1858. Finally, in 1860 he was elected President of the United States. These were just a few rough spots in the life of Abraham Lincoln.

Nothing in the world can take the place of persistence. Talent will not. Nothing is more common than talented people who are unsuccessful. Genius will not. Unrewarded genius is almost a proverb. Education alone will not. The world is full of educated derelicts. Persistence and determination alone are omnipotent.

Everything changes in this universe. There is nothing we can do about it. Governments change. Maybe you will wake up in the morning to a new president or a new king, or to a revolution somewhere. Everything is in a state of flux.

When faced with major setbacks, it is tempting to give up and succumb to depression, but always remember the old legend about King Solomon.

Feeling blue, the king asked his advisors to find him a ring he had once seen in a dream.

"When I feel satisfied, I'm afraid that it won't last. And when I don't, I am afraid my sorrow will go on forever. Find me the ring that will ease my suffering," he demanded.

Solomon sent out all of his advisors, and eventually one of them met an old jeweler who carved into a simple gold band the inscription "This too shall pass." When the king received his ring and read the inscription, his sorrows turned to joy and his joy to sorrows, and then both gave way to equanimity.

Yes, your current problem shall pass away. You can't be frustrated forever. And there is something you and I can do about our attitude toward these constant changes. It's not what happens, it is what we think about what happens that matters.

All endeavors cannot succeed. Interspersed with the joy of success is the bitterness of failure. By dealing with failures constructively, we can often turn those failures into successes.

The lowest point in Lee Iacocca's career was when he was fired from the Ford Motor Company. How he turned his defeat into success in his new job as CEO of Chrysler is well known. In his autobiography he reported that immediately upon starting his new job, he was faced with an even more devastating defeat. Chrysler was on the verge of bankruptcy. A lesser person might have quit right then, rather than move from one failure to another.

Iacocca refused to let this defeat him. He called on all his inner resources. He had tasted failure before, and this time he wasn't going to let it push him down. He channeled his strengths in adaptability, innovation, creative thinking, and perseverance to confront this crisis and beat it.

The Master Thoughts

Attitudes are the immaterial stuff of which we build ability, equanimity, and prosperity. They are how we direct our lives, and our changed attitudes can change everything else. What is your attitude of mind? These, of course, are master thoughts, which can bring about great and wonderful experiences and results. Because when you change your mind you change your body, for your body is a shadow of the mind. Your body is the mind condensed. It is done unto you as you believe.

It is negative thinking that keeps so many people from being resilient when things go wrong. They won't let their subconscious mind open up to making necessary adaptations and changes.

Your master thoughts enable you to overcome this negativity. You can if you think you can. You have within you the seed of resilience and you can germinate that seed through the Infinite Power that strengthens you. Nearly everyone knows how impossible it is to fight a domineering, negative thought or emotion; but you can. When the negative thought comes to you—fear, resentment, condemnation, hate, or whatever it might be—deal with it immediately. Decapitate it. Don't let it grow up and become strong, challenge your dominion, defeat you, and give you sickness and failure. Because if the resentment grows in your mind, it begins to dominate you; then you color everything in your life with fear. It colors everything you do, say, and think, and in addition, it keeps you from using your creativity to innovate and adapt to new situations.

It is said that Thomas Edison failed in his attempt to develop the incandescent bulb one thousand times before he succeeded, but he never let negative thoughts stop him from continuing to adapt and fine-tune the process. As noted earlier in this chapter, Lee Iacocca utilized his adaptability and creativity to convince Congress to provide the funds that saved Chrysler from bankruptcy.

Expand Your Inner Resources

Men and women who are trying to make the most of their lives never stop growing. They are always on the road because their goal is always receding, as they grow larger, broader, and more efficient. They only stop off at way stations to unpack a few things they no longer need, impediments that hamper them, and then they resume their journey. This is the way all along the life path.

If you want to get at your hidden resources, stimulate your growth and your power, you must be continually improving yourself somewhere; increasing your intelligence by closer and keener observation, by the constant improving of your knowledge, the broadening of your mental and spiritual outlook, the getting away from self, and the enlarging of your sphere of service and helpfulness. Stop fearing change. Be confident in your ability to meet challenges with new and imaginative ideas.

The CEO of Burberry, Angela Ahrendts, attributes her success to observing and emulating top people in her field. She said she learned her quantitative skills from Linda Wachner, who headed the apparel giant Warnaco, and her creative skills from another fashion leader, Donna Karan. Linda was an expert on the numbers, and Donna taught her a great deal about design.

Earlier in her career, she had left Donna Karan's company to help open fifty Bendel stores around the United States. But after eighteen months the board canceled the project, which Ahrendts describes as "the most devastating blow in my career." She quickly bounced back, however, when she was hired at Liz Claiborne. At this firm she was able to use both her business and creative skills to convince them to expand by buying Juicy Couture, which Karan's people had been reluctant to do.

When the long-term CEO of Burberry, an international chain of boutiques, retired, Ahrendts was hired to replace her. Her innovative concepts and her commitment to accepting new ideas have successfully enabled the company to expand and prosper.

When you are overwrought with problems, think of the secret chambers of possibilities that were unlocked in a multitude of people like Angela Ahrendts. There are thousands of people living today who are grander men and women, better husbands and wives, better lawyers, better physicians, better statesmen because of having met challenges similar to Ahrendts's. There is no other means of self-discovery so potent as an inspiring book or listening to a great orator. This often stirs us to the very centers of our being and awakens new impulses and new determination in many of us who up to that time had been asleep so far as knowing and utilizing our inner powers were concerned. Perhaps you have had this experience in listening to some great preacher or lecturer who seemed to open up realms in your nature that otherwise might have remained forever hidden.

The more highly we cultivate all our faculties, the more deeply we draw upon our resources, the more of our hidden selves we discover, the wider our vision grows. Life becomes perpetual progress.

There are people who never realized their possibilities until they reached middle life. Then they were suddenly aroused, as if from a long sleep, by reading some inspiring, stimulating book, by listening to a sermon or a lecture, or by meeting some friend—someone with high ideals—who understood, believed in, and encouraged them.

It will make all the difference in the world to you whether you are with people who are watching for ability in you, people who believe in, encourage, and praise you, or whether you are with those who are forever breaking your idols, blasting your hopes, and throwing cold water on your aspirations.

A good example of this is Andrea Wong, president and CEO of Lifetime Television. She says it was important for her parents to let her fail as she was growing up. That gave her a lot of strength. When she lost the school elections for class president, she learned to dust herself off and keep going. She brought this into her career in the hectic television production field, where for every hit, there are untold numbers of programs that never see the light of day. When she conceived the idea of bringing the British TV show *Dancing with the Stars* to the United States, people in the industry thought she was crazy, but she believed in it and persuaded the network to air it. It became one of the most watched programs that year. In her new role as head of her own network, her challenge is to grow the Lifetime brand, and to do that, she calls on the mental confidence she started developing as a child and her continuing efforts to learn and improve.

Learn from Your Failures

If you interview the great army of failures, you will find that multitudes have failed because they never got into a stimulating, encouraging environment, because their ambition was never aroused, or because they were not strong enough to rally under depressing, discouraging, or vicious surroundings. Most of the people we find in prisons and poorhouses are examples of the influence of an environment that appealed to the worst instead of to the best in them.

Whatever you do in life, make any sacrifice necessary to keep in an ambition-arousing atmosphere, an environment that will stimulate you to self-development. Keep close to the people who understand you, who believe in you, who will help you to discover yourself and encourage you to make the most of yourself. This may make all the difference to you between a grand success and a mediocre existence. Stick to those who are trying to do something and to be somebody in the world—people of high aims, lofty ambition. Ambition is contagious. You will catch the spirit that dominates in your environment. The success of those about you who are trying to climb upward will encourage and stimulate you to struggle harder if you have not done quite so well yourself.

Nicholas Hall knows that failure is a relative term. He puts failure right in his company name. A serial entrepreneur, he's the founder of StartupFailures.com, a popular website started to record the adventures of entrepreneurship. He says that succeeding involves bouncing back and overcoming self-doubt. He considers failure a close relative of success, and is intimately familiar with both. He also provides encouragement and advice on how to get back on track.

Hall's core belief is that *the only real failure comes from not trying*. He also says that failure comes with the territory, that anyone who has ever had success, either personal or professional, has also had failures. He says only the willingness to bounce back gives you the chance to go to bat again.

Even if a startup is successful, he doesn't know any founder who hasn't faced actual or perceived failure plenty of times in getting there . . . even the Microsofts and the Apples! He admits that plenty of people starting businesses understand that failure is part of the process, but they just hope that they can skip that part.

The biggest hurdle to bouncing back is self-doubt. But one comforting thought is that though failure may not become easier to take over time, bouncing back seems to become easier to do.

The trick is to see it as just part of the process, the key to staying in the game.

SUM AND SUBSTANCE

- You do not have to go along with negative thoughts or reactions. Begin to positively refuse to react mechanically. React and think in a new way. You want to be peaceful, happy, radiant, healthy, prosperous, and inspired. From this moment forward, refuse to identify with the negative thoughts that tend to drag you down.

- Don't fear change. Don't be held back because you think your boss or others will not agree. Be prepared to adapt, to create, to amend, to hone your ideas to meet challenges on the job.

- Nothing in the world can take the place of persistence. Talent will not. Nothing is more common than talented people who are unsuccessful. Genius will not. Unrewarded genius is almost a proverb. Education alone will not. The world is full of educated derelicts. Persistence and determination alone are omnipotent.

- When the negative thought comes to you, deal with it immediately. Don't let it defeat you. If the resentment grows in your mind, it begins to dominate you; then you color everything in your life with fear.

- By constantly thinking of positive approaches to solving problems, and feeding your subconscious mind with thoughts of flexibility and willingness to adapt, you will overcome your fears of making changes and build up resistance to negative thinking.

- Whatever you do in life, make any sacrifice necessary to remain in an environment that will stimulate you to self-development.

Keep close to the people who understand you, who believe in you, who will help you discover yourself and encourage you to make the most of yourself. This may make all the difference between a grand success and a mediocre existence.

• Failures may happen, but don't let them destroy you. Everything passes. It's not what happens, it is what we think about what happens that matters.

Chapter Seven

Overcoming Worry and Stress

All the water in the ocean will not sink even a small boat if the water doesn't get inside the boat; likewise all the problems, challenges, and difficulties in the world cannot sink you, as long as you do not permit them to get inside you.

Prolonged worry robs you of vitality, enthusiasm, and energy, leaving you a physical and mental wreck. Medical professionals point out that chronic worry is behind numerous diseases such as asthma, allergies, cardiac trouble, high blood pressure, and a host of other illnesses too numerous to mention.

The worried mind is confused and divided, and is thinking aimlessly about a lot of things that are not true. Although many of us have real troubles, such as illness in our family or the loss of a job, much worry is due to indolence, laziness, apathy, and indifference. When you wake up, you do not have to think worrisome thoughts. You can think of harmony, peace, beauty, right action, love, and understanding. You can supplant the negative thought with a constructive thought.

Steve L. had been worried about his health, but after a comprehensive physical exam, his doctor told him there was nothing wrong with him physically, but that he was suffering from anxiety neurosis. Anxiety neurosis is a fancy phrase for just plain, chronic worry. And the word "worry," when you translate it from its original root, means "to strangle, to choke," which is what Steve was doing to himself.

He was also constantly worrying about money, his job, and the future. His vision of success and prosperity was thwarted by his chronic worry, and the fretting consumed his energy. He felt constantly tired and depressed.

He was advised to have quiet sessions with himself three or four times a day and declare solemnly that the Almighty had given him inspiration and hope and all he needed to do was tune in on the Infinite and let the harmony, peace, and love of that source move through him. The following meditation was recommended:

> God, or the Supreme Wisdom, gave me this desire. The Almighty Power is within me, enabling me to be, to do, and to have. This Wisdom and Power of the Almighty backs me up and enables me to fulfill all my goals. I no longer think about obstacles, delays, impediments, and failure. I know that thinking constantly along this line builds up my faith and confidence and increases my strength and poise, for God hath not given us the spirit of fear but of power, and of love, and of a sound mind.

He meditated on these words regularly and systematically. These truths entered into his conscious mind, and then his brain sent these healing vibrations all over his system. They went into his subconscious mind and, like spiritual penicillin, they destroyed the bacteria of worry, fear, anxiety, and all those negative thoughts. In a month's time he arrived at that awareness of strength, power, and intelligence that was implanted in him at birth. He has conquered his worries by partaking of the spiritual medicine and Infinite Intelligence locked in the subconscious depths.

Break Your Worries into Pieces

Andy F., an engineer, reported that he looks at his worries as an engineering problem. "When I face a technical problem on the job," he said, "I take it apart and break it into small pieces. Then I ask myself 'Where do they come from? What does each piece signify? How can I adapt it to the entire problem?' With worries I ask, 'Do these worries have any power?' Is there any principle behind them?' "

With his cool, rational thought and logical analysis, he dismembers his worries and realizes they are shadows in his mind, fallacious and illusionary. No reality, just shadows in the mind.

A shadow has no power! Well, that's what much worry is: a shadow in your mind. It has no reality, no principle behind it, and no truth behind it. These worries are no more than a conglomeration of sinister shadows. Eliminate those shadows by converting them into realities and dealing with them.

Your Body Reflects What Is in Your Mind

Doctors will tell you that many of their patients worry so much about diseases that they do *not* have, that they suffer the symptoms of those ailments. Doctors call these symptoms "psychosomatic." The roots of this word are *psycho*, which means "of the mind," and *somatic*, meaning "of the body." What you think in your mind is reflected by the reaction of your body.

The vice president of a major insurance company in Hartford, Connecticut, was worried that he had a bad heart. His closest friend, a man twenty years older than he, had just had a heart attack and he was sure that he was also susceptible. He went to see a heart specialist, who took a cardiogram and learned that his heart was normal and that his problem was psychosomatic. His friend's heart attack triggered in him an inordinate concern about his own heart and he actually experienced spasms in his chest and other symptoms of heart trouble. The doctor told him that the cure for his problem was not in medical books, but in his subconscious mind. He prescribed that he meditate on good health until the false idea was lifted from his *psyche*, and then his *soma* would respond. It only took a few weeks. He practiced the great law of substitution by repeating the good idea over and over again until the mind accepted the truth, which set him free and left him serene.

It takes a little work, but you can do it. It is a discipline. It's a willingness to do it. "I'm going to overcome this. I'm going to meet it head-on. It's a shadow in my mind, and I'm not going to give power to shadows." The insurance executive's emotional spasms were caused because he was obsessed with the idea that he had a bad heart. He didn't. So he was completely healed. He was healed of what? A false belief in his own mind.

The Power Is Within You

Whenever any fear or worry comes to you, or whenever you think you cannot accomplish something, get still and quiet and recognize that Infinity is within you, that God is boundless love, Infinite Intelligence, Infinite Life, marvelous wisdom, absolute power, absolute harmony.

If you call upon It, It answers you. Infinite Intelligence responds to your thought. This type of prayer or meditation will bring about complete relaxation, quiet your mind. When in this relaxed state of being, contemplate what you want to be, to do, or to have, and the Infinite Spirit within you will respond to your faith and confidence in it. This faith will filter down into your subconscious and enhance this powerful force in coping with any problems you face.

For years Carlos J. drew charts and graphs for the marketing department of his company. As he was praised over and over again for the clarity and accuracy of his work, Carlos felt very secure in his job. But as computer techniques developed, there was no longer a need for a person with Carlos's skill. Instead of whining about unfairness or griping about his bad luck, Carlos persuaded his company to retrain him in computer graphics. He studied hard and mastered the new techniques. He learned that his previous charting experience gave him much insight in computer graphics, and he mastered the subject and became a top performer.

Let nothing bother you, let nothing frighten you, let nothing disturb you, let nothing anger you. You are a master. You are in charge of your own conceptive realm: of your thoughts, feelings, emotions, and reactions. You are a king over your own conceptive realm. When any negative suggestion comes to you, you can say, "I have within me the capability and strength to overcome this. With the help of the Infinite Power, I will be able to find an answer to this."

Feed Positive Thoughts into Your Conscious Mind

Worry and fear can only dominate your life if you let them. You have the power to eliminate them from your life. You have the Presence within you, the strength to change your life. By prayer and meditation, by commitment to your spiritual self, by trust in the Divine, you will overcome your fears and concerns. If you feed positive thoughts into your conscious mind, your subconscious mind will respond positively when faced with problems, and find solutions that will result in a happier, more peaceful, and more rewarding life.

Many people fail by constantly stopping to wonder how they will finally come out, whether they will succeed or not. This constant questioning of the outcome of things creates doubt, which is fatal to achievement.

The secret of achievement, whether it be on your job or in other aspects of your life, is concentration. Worry or fear of any kind is fatal to mental concentration and kills creative ability. One of the most common reasons workers suffer on a job is the fear caused by a domineering boss—a boss who constantly threatens to punish, even fire, workers who displease him or her. It is never easy to work under such circumstances, and many people are constantly miserable in them. Their whole mental organism vibrates with conflicting emotions, and efficiency is impossible.

It's unlikely that you can change your boss's personality, but you can learn to live with it without letting it wear you down. Every time you catch yourself worrying or fretting or being anxious about this treatment, just pause for a few moments and say to yourself, "This is not living the life of an intelligent, thinking being, not the life of a real person." Of course, if it is possible to change jobs either within the organization or by leaving it, do so. But if this is not an option, whenever your boss berates you, repeat to yourself: "I will not let this ruin my life. I will maintain my equanimity on the job and know that I am doing my best despite the attitude of my boss. I will not let this drag me down." This thinking may not alleviate the situation, but it will enable you to accept it and seek areas outside the job to attain satisfaction and achievement.

Relax Your Body, Quiet Your Mind

You are scheduled for your annual performance review with your boss tomorrow morning. What do you do? You will probably worry about what your boss will say. You will recall all of the errors you've made, the deadlines missed, or other problems. Your subconscious mind may be burdened with negativity that will keep you from sleeping that night.

But instead, let's assume that you know the laws of mind and the way of the spirit. Instead of worrying about the review, you sit down in your chair or on your couch and mobilize your attention. You relax first. When the body is relaxed, the mind becomes quiet. You say to yourself, "My toes are relaxed, my feet are relaxed, my abdominal muscles are relaxed, my heart and lungs are relaxed, my spine is relaxed, my neck is relaxed, my hands and arms are relaxed, my brain is relaxed, my eyes are relaxed, my whole being is completely relaxed from head to foot."

When you are relaxed, your body has to obey you; when you relax and believe, your prayer is always answered. If you do not relax, you do not get results. *Relax and believe.* When you relax your body, you are relaxing your mind. Your mind becomes quiet and still. So what would you do to prepare for what has always been an ordeal for you? You should concentrate on all your accomplishments over the past year—the costs you reduced, the innovations you suggested, the customers you satisfied, and all the other positive actions you were involved in. If you run that movie in your mind and keep it up, you will be ready.

When you meet with your boss the next morning, you will go in with a strong positive attitude. Worry will have been replaced with confidence. Sure, the boss may point to areas in which improvement can be made. That's your boss's job, and all of us can make improvements. But you will accept them as constructive suggestions not as criticism. You will have programmed your subconscious to replace concern and worry about your job with the assurance that you are doing well and are willing and able to do even better.

You Think You Have Problems?

There is an old tale about a wise man, a lover of the mysteries of life, a mystic, who instructed all the people on earth to form a great circle. In the center of the circle they were to deposit all their problems, grievances, misunderstandings, heartbreaks, ailments, lacks, and limitations—problems of all manner and every kind.

Then they were granted permission, indeed they were ordered, ordained, to examine the whole sorry lot (this conglomeration of difficulties) and to select any of them they wished for their own. A great hush fell over the multitudes. They became very still and quiet.

After much thought and due deliberation, every man and every woman went back to the center of the circle and each one retrieved his or her problems, and returned home. No one, not one soul, elected to select, choose, or take onto his or her shoulders the burdens, distresses, trials, and tribulations of another.

It is so tempting to attempt to solve the problems of others. It is a fallacy and a complete waste and dissipation of our energies. With all the goodwill and intentions in the world, much as we might desire to—we are not competent to resolve the conditions of another.

But it is only we, ourselves, who are ultimately equipped to cope with our own lives—for they are of our creation. We can alter and improve them by changing our beliefs, remembering who we truly are. We must continually remind ourselves to accept our legacy, our inheritance, of all that is good and true and beautiful.

Beat the Blues

There are times in the lives of most people when things go awry on the job. Work piles up. Deadlines are missed. No matter how hard you work, you never seem to catch up. You get depressed.

When you feel this depression coming on, concentrate your mind vigorously upon the very opposite qualities. Remember that you have faced crises in your work in the past and have overcome them. Hold the ideals of cheerfulness, confidence, gratitude, goodwill toward everybody, and you will be surprised to see how quickly the enemies who were dogging your steps and making your life miserable will disappear, just as the darkness does when the shutters are opened and the light rushes in. We do not drive out the darkness, but introduce its antidote, light, which instantly neutralizes it. When the pressure is on to meet a deadline, when the boss rejects your work on a project and demands you redo it, when you lose a sale that you needed to meet your quota, and everything seems to be going wrong and you feel the "blues" getting a grip on you, stop whatever you are doing and make a business of driving these enemies out of your mind, neutralizing them, killing them, with their opposite suggestions. You know perfectly well that a cheerful, beautiful thought, no matter how difficult it may be for you to hold when you are suffering, will soon bring you relief. Assume the cheerful, hopeful virtue if you have it not, and it will soon be yours.

If you are a victim of your moods, push right into the swim of things and take an active part, with a real interest in what is going on around you. Take a respite from your job problems. A short break often refreshes the mind and helps you think more clearly when you return. Be happy, and interest yourself in others. Keep your mind off yourself. Get away from yourself by entering with zest into plans with friends or family, or the plans and pleasures of others about you.

Don't focus on your immediate concerns. Think back on your successes and how you achieved them. Recall that tough assignment that you solved when others had given up. Remember how your boss praised your creativity, your diligence, and your loyalty in the past. Dwell on victories rather than agonize over failures. This will clear your mind and help you develop approaches to solve current problems.

Don't estimate your future by the little troubles that confront you now. The black clouds that shut out your sun today will be gone tomorrow. Learn to look at life at long range and to put the right values upon things.

You are the master of your thought reactions. You can order your thoughts around as you like, giving attention to whatever you choose to meditate on. You are a monarch in your conceptual realm. You can order your subjects—thoughts and feelings—according to your desires, and they must obey you. You are the absolute monarch in your mental kingdom, with power to eliminate all enemies from your realm.

Worry and fear are false beliefs of the mind. False beliefs will die if you refuse to give them attention. Worry of any kind is nature's alarm signal that you believe wrongly. A change of thought will set you free. People who worry always expect things to go wrong. They will tell you all the reasons why something bad could happen, and not one reason why something good should or could happen. Such worry makes them weaker and less able to meet any challenges that might come along, as they attract exactly the conditions upon which they are mentally dwelling.

The fearful, worrisome perspective we impress upon our subconscious minds practically guarantees that some corresponding challenge or difficulty will erupt.

Here are nine ways to reduce stress and worry on the job:

1. *Learn to relax*. Set up periods of time during the workday when you can spend a few minutes by yourself to engage in deep meditation or programmed relaxation exercises. A short break often refreshes the mind and helps you think more clearly when you return.

2. *Take a walk*. If you can get away from your desk or cubicle, take a walk. Go out of the building. Walk around the block or the parking lot. Get some fresh air. If you are restricted to the building, walk inside. Removing yourself from the place of stress often helps alleviate the stress.

3. *Believe in yourself*. Don't let pressure or criticism from others control your emotions.

4. *Explore your spirituality*. Whenever you begin to feel stressed, call on your religious or spiritual beliefs to guide you toward peace of mind.

5. *Keep learning*. The experience of ongoing learning keeps you alert, open-minded, and stimulated.

6. *Develop a support team.* Avoid major stress by having friends and team members available to back you up when things don't go well.

7. *Accept only commitments that are important to accomplishing the mission of your job.* Politely turn down other projects that drain your time and energy.

8. *Seek new ways of using your creativity.* By rethinking the way you perform routine tasks, you make them less boring and stressful. By developing creative approaches to new assignments, you make them less stressful to handle.

9. *Welcome changes.* Consider them new challenges rather than threats to the status quo.

SUM AND SUBSTANCE

- When you worry about your job, you often brood over a great many things that never will happen, and you deplete yourself of vitality, enthusiasm, and energy.

- If you sustain the worry habit, you may attract what you are worrying about.

- Worry and fear are false beliefs of the mind. False beliefs will die if you refuse to give them attention. Worry of any kind is nature's alarm signal that you believe wrongly. A change of thought will set you free.

Chapter Eight

Conquering Fear

When faced with an abnormal fear, place your attention on the thing immediately desired. Get absorbed and engrossed in your desire. This attitude will give you confidence and lift your spirits. The infinite power of your subconscious mind is moving on your behalf. It cannot fail. Therefore, peace and assurance are yours. The fear of failure itself creates the experience of failure.

Most of us worry about problems that develop in our work and our lives, and as noted in the previous chapter, we can learn to cope with it. However, there are times when problems seem too burdensome and we just cannot face them. Fear has replaced confidence in our subconscious minds.

Fear is the most extensive of all the morbid mental conditions that reflect themselves so disastrously in the human system. It has many degrees or gradations, from the state of extreme alarm, fright, or terror, down to the slightest shade of apprehension of impending evil. But all along the line it is the same thing—a paralyzing impression upon the centers of life, which can produce, through the agency of the nervous system, a vast variety of morbid symptoms in every tissue of the body.

Fear is like carbonic-acid gas pumped into one's atmosphere. It causes mental, moral, and spiritual asphyxiation, and sometimes death—death to energy, death to tissue, and death to all growth.

Countless people suffer from the dread of some impending evil. It haunts them even in their happiest moments. Their happiness is poisoned with it so that they never take much pleasure or comfort in anything. It is the ghost at the banquet, the skeleton in the closet. It is ingrained into their very lives and emphasized in their excessive timidity, their shrinking, and their self-conscious bearing.

We often fear that decisions we make on the job will result in failure, criticism from the boss, demotion, or even termination. This can lead to headaches, ulcers, and emotional problems. Fear is one of the greatest causes of misery on the job, failure to advance in one's career, and even getting fired.

Fear Can Dominate Your Life

Worry, anxiety, anger, jealousy, and timidity are early symptoms of fear. Unless they are identified and dealt with, they will metastasize into fear. Fear is a major cause of unhappiness and inefficiency, and has made more people cowards and failures, and forced more of them into mediocrity, than anything else.

All work done when one is suffering from a sense of fear or foreboding has little efficiency. Fear strangles originality, daring, boldness; it kills individuality and weakens all the mental processes. Great things are never done under a sense of fear of some impending danger. Fear always indicates weakness, the presence of cowardice. It is a slaughterer of years, a sacrificer of happiness and ambitions, and a ruiner of careers.

Fear depresses normal mental action, and renders one incapable of acting wisely in an emergency, for no one can think clearly and act wisely when paralyzed by fear. When you become melancholy and discouraged about your affairs, when you are filled with fear that you are going to fail and are haunted by the specter of poverty and a suffering family, before you realize it you attract the very things you dread.

There is no need to fear. Tell this to yourself over and over again. Gradually, your subconscious will accept it. And your subconscious will believe it, because you believe it in your conscious, reasoning mind. Whatever your conscious mind really believes, your subconscious will dramatize and bring to manifestation. Do not vacillate or equivocate. Your subconscious mind knows when you are sincere. It knows when you really believe; then, it will respond. If instead of giving up to fear, you persist in keeping prosperity in mind, assume a hopeful, optimistic attitude, and conduct your business in a systematic, economical, farsighted manner, actual failure will be comparatively rare.

Change Your Thoughts from Fear to Faith

We have the capacity to easily destroy fear by simply changing the thought. Fear depresses, suppresses, strangles. If it is indulged in, it will change a positive, creative mental attitude into a nonproductive, negative one, and this is fatal to achievement. The effect of fear, especially where the fear thought has become habitual, is to dry up the very source of life. Faith that replaces fear has just the opposite effect upon the body and brain. It enlarges, opens up the nature, gives abundant life to the cells, and increases the brainpower.

Fear wreaks terrible havoc with the imagination, which pictures all sorts of dire things. Faith is its perfect antidote, for while fear sees only the darkness and the shadows, faith sees the silver lining, the sun behind the cloud. Fear looks down and expects the worst; faith looks up and anticipates the best. Fear is pessimistic; faith is optimistic. Fear always predicts failure; faith predicts success. There can be no fear of poverty or failure when the mind is dominated by faith. Doubt cannot exist in its presence. It is above all adversity.

Andrew L. was a highly talented violinist. He was the best violinist in his high school orchestra, and his teachers encouraged him to pursue a concert career. Andrew had no problem playing his best in an orchestra and playing solo to a small audience. Then, when the school orchestra was awarded the honor of performing a Beethoven violin concerto at a large concert hall, Andrew was chosen to play the violin solo. He performed beautifully in the rehearsals, but on the night of the concert, when he faced an auditorium filled to capacity, Andrew froze. He was so consumed with fear that he could not play and had to be escorted off the stage.

From that moment on, Andrew refused to play. He chose to pursue another career, but always dreamed of living a life of music. Could Andrew's musical career have been salvaged? Of course it could have. Other men and women have overcome stage fright to become great actors, musicians, singers, and orators. They refused to let one or even several defeats stop them. They had faith in themselves.

A powerful faith is a great asset because it never frets; it sees beyond the temporary annoyance, the discord, the trouble; it sees the sun behind the cloud. It knows things will come out right, because it sees the goal that the eye cannot see.

Overcoming Fear

In setting about the overcoming of fear, we must first understand what it is we fear. It is always something that has not yet happened— it is nonexistent. Trouble is an imaginary something that we think of, and which frightens us with its possibility.

Most people are afraid to walk on a narrow place high above the ground. If that same narrow space were marked on the floor or a room, they could keep within it perfectly, and never think of losing their balance. The most dangerous thing about walking in such a place is the fear of falling. Steady-headed people are simply fearless; they do not allow the thought of possible danger to overcome them, but keep their physical powers under perfect control. An acrobat has only to conquer fear to perform most of the feats that astound spectators.

Take a very common fear—that of losing one's job. The people who make their lives miserable worrying about this possible misfortune have not lost their jobs; they are suffering nothing; there is no danger of want. The present situation is therefore satisfactory. If dismissal comes, it is then too late to worry about it coming, and all previous worrying will have been pure waste, doing no good, but rather weakening one for the necessary struggle to get placed again. The thing worried about then will tend to be that another place will not be found. If a place is found, all the worrying will again have been useless. Under no circumstances can the worrying be justified by the situation at any particular time. Its object is always an imaginary situation of the future.

In overcoming your various fears, follow each one out to its logical conclusion and convince yourself that at the present moment the things you fear do not exist outside of your imagination. Whether they ever come to pass in the future or not, your fear is a waste of time, energy, and actual bodily and mental strength. Quit worrying just as you would quit eating or drinking something you felt sure had caused you pain in the past. If you must worry about something, worry about the terrible effects of worrying; it may help you to a cure.

If the fear is of personal failure, instead of thinking how little and weak you are, how ill-prepared for the great task, and how

---

Merely convincing yourself that what you fear is imaginary will not suffice until you have trained your mind to throw off suggestions of fear, and to combat all thought that leads to it. This means constant watchfulness and alert mental effort. When the thoughts of foreboding or worry begin to suggest themselves, do not indulge them and let them grow big and black. Change your thought to the affirmative, positive actions you can take.

sure you are to fail, think how strong and competent you are, how you have successfully done similar tasks, and how you are going to utilize all your past experience and rise to this present occasion, do the task triumphantly, and be ready for a bigger one. It is an attitude such as this, whether consciously assumed or not, that carries one to higher and yet higher places. This same principle of crowding out the fear by a buoyant, hopeful, confident thought can be applied to all the many kinds of fear that daily and hourly beset us.

Just as fear can debilitate you, the act of overcoming fear can prod you to great achievement. One rainy and windy day, a long-legged medical student was worried. He had a race to run, and fear had turned him pale. He would be described later as looking like a man going to the electric chair or like a man being tortured. His coach had the same fears about the weather, but kept them to himself as they sat opposite each other on the train. The runner feared that the wind, which had picked up, would add a critical one second to each of his four laps. The coach knew the damage that kind of doubt could do to an athlete, so he assured the runner that yes, he had the legs to do what he had to do . . . that is, with the proper motivation, with a good reason for wanting to do it. He told the fearful runner that his mind could overcome any adversity, and that he knew a great athlete in Ireland who won a tough race without training or proper food, just the will to run. And what, the coach asked, if this were your only chance? The runner would later say that he had needed the coach to tell him he could do it. He just needed to hear that booming voice say what he hoped was his inner truth: that he could meet this greatest of challenges, despite conditions. The coach, Fritz Stampfl, would later write that a runner's greatest asset, apart from fitness, is a cool and calculating brain allied to confidence and courage. He should know: He had just given Roger Bannister the courage to break the four-minute mile.

Take Charge of Your Mind

We must learn to establish control over our thoughts, feelings, and responses. We must not let fear make decisions for us. We must take charge and say to fears, "I am the master, I am going to order my thoughts around, I am not afraid to make this decision." Tell your mind what to give attention to, then you'll be like an employer ordering employees to execute his or her instructions.

You must take charge of your own mind; not permit others to govern it for you. Creed, dogma, traditions, superstition, fear, and ignorance rule the mind of the average person. The greatest desert in the world is not the Sahara; it is in the mind of the average person. Too many people do not own their own minds; they make no effort to think for themselves. They let their minds be ruled over by strong-minded family members at home or governed by the opinions of their bosses or strong-minded coworkers on the job. Do not let this happen to you. Build up the power of your subconscious mind to resist domination by others and assert your ability to control your own destiny.

Examine Your Fears

The head of sales for a major multinational corporation confided that when he first began working as a salesperson, he had to walk around the block five or six times before he could get up the nerve to call on a customer.

His supervisor was both very experienced and very perceptive. One day she said to him, "Don't be afraid of the monster hiding behind the door. There is no monster. You are the victim of a false belief."

The supervisor went on to tell him that whenever she felt the first stirrings of a fear, she stood up to it. She stared it in the face, looking it straight in the eye. When she did that, she always found that her fear faded and shrank into insignificance.

Sarah M.'s boss, Agnes, was a tyrant. She constantly micromanaged the work of all her subordinates. She was quick to criticize, and never praised or even acknowledged good work. Sarah dreaded to go to work and literally trembled when Agnes came close to her work space.

She noticed that Rebecca, a coworker, never seemed fazed by Agnes's diatribes. Sarah asked her how she could remain so serene under such conditions. Rebecca said, "When I first came here, I was terrified by Agnes and was about to quit, but I needed the job. I decided that not Agnes, or anybody else, could ruin my life, unless I let them. I realized that the only person who could make me miserable was me. If I let Agnes make me feel inferior, I will be inferior. So when she berates me, I let it go in one ear and out the other. I block out her negativity and concentrate on the good things in my life. I just nod my head and say, 'Yes, ma'am,' and go on with my work. Try it. It won't happen immediately, but after a while, you'll be able to let Agnes's ranting bounce off you with no effect."

Sarah followed Rebecca's advice. Although the work environment had not changed, her perception of it and her reaction to it made the job more tolerable.

Inspiration Will Bring Victory from Defeat

Perhaps the past has been a bitter disappointment to you. In looking it over, you may feel that you have been a failure, or at best have been plodding along in mediocrity. You may not have succeeded in the particular things you expected to do; you may have lost money when you planned to make it; or you may have lost friends and relatives who were very dear to you. You may have lost your business, and even your home may have been wrenched from you because you could not pay the mortgage on it, or because of sickness and consequent inability to work. A serious accident may have apparently robbed you of power. The new year may present a very discouraging outlook to you. Yet, in spite of any or all of these misfortunes, if you refuse to be conquered, victory is awaiting you farther along the road.

There is no need to feel inferior if you lose courage and are afraid to face the world just because you have made a mistake or a slip, because your business has failed, because your property has been swept away by some general disaster, or because of other trouble impossible for you to have averted.

This is the test of your courage: How much is there left in you after you have lost everything outside of yourself? If you lie down now, throw up your hands, and acknowledge yourself bested, there is not much in you. But if, with heart undaunted and face turned forward, you refuse to give up or to lose faith in yourself, if you scorn to beat a retreat, you will show you are bigger than your loss, greater than your burdens, and larger than any defeat.

You may say that you have failed too often, that there is no use in trying, that it is impossible for you to succeed, and that you have fallen too often even to attempt to get on your feet again. Nonsense! There is no failure for a person whose spirit is unconquered. No matter how late the hour or how many and repeated your failures, success is still possible. Time and again in the history of our daily lives, chronicled in our newspapers, recorded in biographies, or exhibited before our eyes, we see men and women redeeming past failures, rising up out of the stupor of discouragement, and boldly turning face forward once more.

If you are made of the stuff that wins, if you have grit and nerve in you, your misfortunes, losses, and defeats will call them out and make you all the stronger. "It is defeat," said the Rev. Henry Ward Beecher, "that turns bone to flint and gristle to muscle and makes us invincible."

One must come up again and again and wrest triumph from defeat. That is the secret of the success of every brave and noble life that ever was lived.

How many times we come to a crisis in life when some obstacle confronts us that we think will be a terrible calamity and will perhaps ruin us if we cannot avoid it! We fear that our ambition will be thwarted, or that our lives, perhaps, will be wrecked. The dread of the shock that we think will overwhelm us as we come nearer and nearer to it, without any possibility of averting it, is something frightful.

Some people get along beautifully for half a lifetime, perhaps, while everything goes smoothly. While they are accumulating property and gaining friends and reputation, their characters seem to be strong and well balanced; but the moment trouble comes, a failure in business, a panic, or a great crisis in which they lose their all—they are overwhelmed. They despair, lose heart, courage, faith, hope, and power to try again—everything. Fear seeps down into their subconscious mind and dominates their personality.

Let everything else go, if you must, but never lose your grip on yourself. Do not succumb to fear. Replace it with hope. Cling to it with all your might. You are so much greater than any material failure that can come to you, that it would scarcely be mentioned in your biography, and would be regarded as a mere incident in your career—inconvenient, but not very important.

SUM AND SUBSTANCE

- Fear and worry make us attract the very things we dread. The fear habit impairs health, shortens life, and paralyzes efficiency. Doubt and fear mean failure; faith is an optimist, fear a pessimist.

- Faith is its perfect antidote, for, while fear sees only the darkness and the shadows, faith sees the silver lining, the sun behind the cloud. Fear looks down and expects the worst; faith looks up and anticipates the best. Fear is pessimistic; faith is optimistic. Fear always predicts failure; faith predicts success.

- Eliminate from your thinking all false beliefs, biases, and superstitions. Order your mind and thoughts to accept whole-heartedly that what you are seeking already exists in the Infinite Mind and all you must do is to identify it mentally and emotionally and it will come to pass.

- Too many people fear to use their own minds. They let their minds be governed by the opinions of their bosses or strong-minded coworkers on the job. Do not let this happen to you. Build up the power of your subconscious mind to resist domination by others and assert your ability to control your own destiny.

- You are so much greater than any material failure that can come to you. No matter what reverses, what disappointments or failures, come to you, you are superior to them. Never lose your equanimity.

Chapter Nine

Enhancing Your Creative Powers

Imagination is your most powerful faculty. Imagine what is lovely and of good report. You are what you imagine yourself to be.

Creativity begins with imagination. We are talking about disciplined, controlled, directed imagination. To image is to conceive something, to impress it on your subconscious mind. Whatever is impressed on the subconscious is expressed on the screen of space as form, function, experience, and event. If you wish to be successful, you must first imagine yourself to be successful. If you wish to be wealthy, you must first imagine yourself as wealthy.

When the world says, "It is impossible; it can't be done," the person with imagination says, "It is done." Imagination can penetrate the depths of reality and reveal the secrets of nature.

Trust Your Imagination
A great industrialist reported how he started in a small store. He said, "I used to dream of a large corporation with branches all over the country." He added that regularly and systematically he pictured in his mind the giant buildings, offices, factories, and stores,

knowing that through the alchemy of the mind he could weave the fabric out of which his dreams would be clothed. He prospered and began to attract to himself by the universal law of attraction the ideas, personnel, friends, money, and everything needed for the development of his ideal.

So this man truly exercised his imagination and lived with these mental patterns of mind until imagination clothed them in form. He concluded, "It is just as easy to imagine yourself successful as it is to imagine failure; and it's far more interesting."

Whatever you can conceive, you can give it conception. You impregnate your subconscious mind with the picture of the idea, the ideal. The soul, the ancients said, can see invisible things in your mind. Where is the invention? Where is the new play? Where is that secret invention of yours now? It's in your mind. It is real. It has form, shape, and substance in another dimension of mind. Believe you have it now, and you shall receive it.

Imagination—The Seed of Action

A good example of how one man's imagination created one of the most successful businesses is Howard Schultz, the "Starbucks man." It takes a person with vision, fortitude, and unswerving confidence to make a new concept succeed.

Schultz was hired to manage retail sales and marketing for Starbucks, then a small coffee distributor that had a few retail outlets in Seattle. He was twenty-nine, just married. He and his wife left their home in New York City to accept this new job.

About a year later, Schultz visited Italy on a buying trip. As he wandered around Milan, he noticed how important coffee was to the Italian culture. Typically, the workday there starts with a cup of rich coffee at a coffee bar. After work friends and colleagues once again meet at the coffee bar for a leisurely stop before heading home. It was the center of Italian social life. Schultz visualized coffee bars like this transferred to America. It had never been done.

But he felt it could work because of the high quality of Starbucks coffee.

Schultz envisioned hundreds of Starbucks coffee shops across America. Shops businesspeople would stop at on their way to work and come to after work to relax. Shoppers would stop for a pick-me-up. Young people would meet their dates over coffee rather than cocktails. Families would come for refreshment before or after the movies.

It became Schultz's obsession. He was determined to build a national chain of cafés based on the Italian coffee bar, but the Starbucks owners were reluctant. They were in the wholesale coffee bean business; the restaurants they owned were only a small part of their operation.

To implement his goal, Schultz left Starbucks and created a new company. In 1986, he opened his first coffee bar, in Seattle. It was an immediate success. Schultz soon opened another in Seattle and a third in Vancouver. The following year he bought the Starbucks Coffee Company and adopted its name for his enterprise. By the turn of the century, Starbucks had become a basic part of American culture and had expanded to dozens of countries all over the world.

Richard D., a Los Angeles businessman, suffered major financial losses. He prayed for guidance on what steps he should take to move ahead in his life. He had an overpowering feeling that he should go into the desert. While musing there, the idea came to him. He shared this idea with an old acquaintance who ran a successful real estate firm in Los Angeles. He told him the tremendous potential he foresaw in that desert place. He visualized people leaving Los Angeles and coming out from the East to live in what was now just a desert. In his mind's eye, he saw them build homes, hospitals, schools in that place. His friend hired him as a salesman—to promote the development of that desert land. His success led to a partnership in the firm, and today he has become a multimillionaire in real estate.

Believe and You Shall Receive

In your subconscious mind there is an intelligence and wisdom that comes to your aid in emergencies when a direct demand is made upon it. There are many, many such instances where scientists, for example, have received answers to their prayers when they couldn't get an answer any other way.

Nikola Tesla, a brilliant electrical scientist who brought forth the most amazing innovations, said that when an idea for an invention came into his mind, he would build it up in his imagination knowing that his subconscious mind would reconstruct and reveal to his conscious mind all the parts needed for its manufacture in concrete form. Through quietly contemplating every possible improvement, he spent no time in correcting defects and was able to give the technician the perfect product of his mind. He said, "Invariably, my device works as I imagined it should. In twenty years there has not been a single exception." His subconscious mind gave him the answer to all his inventions.

Plato taught that everything exists in ideas or thought images in the mind before it can have external realization. There are false ideas and true ones, a right and a wrong way of thinking. A false or fallacious idea can manifest itself in the body as disease. Robert Fulton's idea became manifested as a steamboat and Samuel Morse's idea as a telegraph. A factory or large department store is the thought of an entrepreneur condensed into objective manifestation.

It is from the realm of imagination that have come television, radio, radar, super jets, and all other modern inventions. Your imagination is the treasure-house of infinity, which releases from your subconscious mind all the precious jewels of music, art, poetry, and invention. You can look at some ancient ruin, an old temple, or a pyramid, and you can reconstruct the records of the dead past. In the ruins of an old churchyard, you also can see a more contemporary city, resurrected in all its former beauty and glory.

Consider for a moment a distinguished, talented architect. He builds in his mind a beautiful, modern city for senior citizens, complete with swimming pools, aquarium, recreation centers, parks, etc. He can construct in his mind the most beautiful palace the human eye has ever seen. He can visualize the buildings in their entirety, completely erected before he *ever* gives his plans to the builders. His inner riches create outer riches for himself and for countless others.

You are the architect of your future. You could now look at an acorn and, with your imaginative eye, construct a magnificent forest full of rivers, streams, and rivulets. You could people the forest with all kinds of life; furthermore, you could hang a bow on every cloud. You could look at a desert and cause it to rejoice and blossom as a rose. People who are gifted with intuition and imagination find water in the desert, and they create cities where formerly others saw only sand and wilderness.

What you imagine as true already exists in your mind, and if you remain faithful to your ideal it will one day objectify itself. The Master Architect within you will project on the screen of visibility that which you impress on your mind.

Imagining Promotes Creativity

Mario A. was a young chemist who worked for a company that had tried to manufacture a certain dye, but had failed. He was given the assignment when they first employed him. He ignored the dye's history of failure and synthesized the compound without any difficulty.

His superiors were amazed and wanted to know his secret. His answer was that he imagined that he had the answer. Pressed further by his superiors, he said that he could clearly see the letters A-N-S-W-E-R in blazing red color in his mind; then he created a vacuum underneath the letters, knowing that as he imagined the chemical formula underneath the letters, his subconscious would fill it in. The third night, he had a dream in which the complete formula and the technique for making the compound were clearly presented. This resulted in a wonderful promotion to an executive capacity in the organization for this young chemist.

Be faithful to the end, full of faith every step of the way, persisting to the finish, and knowing in your heart that the end is secure because you've seen it. Having seen and felt the end, you have willed the means to its realization.

Develop Your Power of Imagination

Creativity is not solely an attribute of artists, inventors, or entrepreneurs. All of us have the power within us. All we need do is develop it and bring it to the surface. Here are some suggestions to help you accomplish this:

1. Imagine yourself doing what you love to do and feel yourself in the act, and wonders will happen in your job and career.

2. Mentally picture yourself as whole and perfect, successful in your career, living in a beautiful home, with a happy, joyous family. Persevere in this mental image, and enjoy the miraculous results.

3. Imagine that your contributions to the company's or department's goals will be recognized by management, and imagine that you are being congratulated on your success.

4. If you focus your mind on situations faced on the job when you are away from your place of work, solutions will often appear complete and ready in your mind without the slightest effort.

5. Visualize in your mind the steps you must take to climb up the career ladder or develop the business you wish to form. Make it vivid, real, natural, dramatic, and exciting. Your subconscious mind will accept what you imagine and feel, and it will bring it to pass.

Edward Harriman imagined a railroad across America. With pen and paper he traced the imaginary line across the continent. The image he had in his mind was backed up by faith and confidence. It revolutionized industry and commerce and put millions to work, making untold fortunes for himself and many others.

Imagine the reality of your desire now and live the role in your imagination. Your inner action must correspond to the action you would physically perform after realizing your desire.

Never Stop Being Creative

Don't let fear of rejection keep you from making creative suggestions. Gary F. pondered an idea he had that could increase productivity by a simple change in methodology. Should he tell his boss? The last time he had made a suggestion, his supervisor rejected it. He said it wouldn't work. Never gave him a chance to explain it. Why bother now?

It is easy to give in to discouragement, but unless you keep coming up with ideas, you will stifle your own creative capabilities. Innovation must be honed by constant use. People tend to censor themselves by worrying about how others will receive their ideas. Self-censorship is far worse than criticism of others because it seeps down into your subconscious mind and makes you feel inadequate. Sure, you will make mistakes; you will make suggestions that don't work; your boss or your coworkers may even ridicule you. Don't let that stop you. Einstein, Edison, Whitney, and Watt were all ridiculed many times. Keep those creative ideas coming.

Honing Your Creativity

There are many ways one can develop creativity. Start by studying existing methods, then ask yourself how they could be made better and use your imagination to find ways to accomplish it. Here are some specific approaches to hone your creative powers:

1. *Observation.* One does not have to dream up ideas to be creative. Observing things around you and applying what you learn to other situations is just as creative as total innovation.

Stan L., manager of Hooper Steel in Las Vegas, noted that as more and more gas stations became "self-service" and no longer had facilities for oil change and lubrication of cars, rapid lubrication stations sprang up to meet this need. Stan used one of them for his car and was pleased with the speed and quality of the work.

For years Hooper Steel had sent its trucks to the service department of the dealer for their regular lubrications. This required sending two people to bring the truck to the dealer (one to drive the other back to the shop in his or her car), leaving the truck at the dealer all day, and returning to pick up the truck—again using the time of two people.

"Why not use the rapid lube station for our trucks?" thought Stan. The result: By sending one driver to the rapid lube station and having that person wait about thirty minutes while the truck was being serviced, Stan saved his company about $1600 a month in out-of-pocket service costs and lost time. In addition they had the use of the truck for most of the day.

2. *Modification.* Can you modify an existing product or concept to create something different? The founders of "Think Big" modified standard products by making enlarged versions of them. Their giant facsimiles of popular products, ranging from pencils

and telephone message pads to animals and furniture, created whole new markets in advertising, decoration, and novelties.

3. *Substitution*. Often inefficiencies can be overcome and problems can be solved by substituting new technologies. But there are many situations when imagination can correct situations more easily and effectively. Darlene A., office manager of Mass.Mailers, was having a difficult time retaining personnel in an extremely dull routine job—stuffing brochures and samples into envelopes. The nature of the job was such that the standard automated equipment could not do it. Not only was the turnover cost expensive, but she could never be sure that workers would be there when needed. She reasoned that although an average employee might find this job boring, perhaps it might be a good opportunity for a mentally challenged person looking to take on new responsibility. She contacted a local group home that worked with mentally challenged individuals, discussed it with the social workers, and arranged to have some of these men and women try the job. This new approach allowed her to hire workers who enjoyed the work and have become steady and valuable employees.

4. *Elimination*. Some of the biggest time wasters and added costs are the result of unnecessary paperwork. As companies grow, the tendency toward bureaucracy and its incumbent proliferation of forms and reports can bog down productivity. Are all these forms really necessary?

Gil W. was irate. His company had added still another form for salespeople to complete. How could he be out there selling when there was so much paperwork? When he complained to his sales manager, she shrugged her shoulders and said they needed the information "upstairs." Gil took all the forms he was required to complete, set them side-by-side, and analyzed what information was involved. It became apparent that there was a good deal of duplication of data. Instead of griping about it, Gil designed a new form that would provide the necessary facts to management and was easy to complete. This not only made the salesperson's job easier, but also saved the company considerable time and money. An added benefit: It started the company on a systematic review of all forms, leading to elimination of many outdated and unnecessary reports.

5. *Adaptation.* Being creative is not limited to coming up with totally original ideas. Creative people often adapt what has worked for others—not necessarily in identical situations—to solve a problem that they are facing.

The North Jersey Limousine Service provides ground transportation from various cities in New Jersey to the major airports in the New York metropolitan area. A constant complaint from their regular customers was about the amount of time they waited when they called for reservations. Each time they had to give their name, address, phone number, credit card number, and other data. One of the executives of the company was a frequent customer of a large mail-order house. He noted that after his first order, he was never again asked for any information other than what he was ordering. He learned that they had a computer database in which all the customer information was placed, and when customers called, they were identified by Caller ID and the file was displayed immediately on the computer screen. By applying this system to North Jersey Limo, they cut the time of taking an order from more than three minutes to twenty-five seconds.

These are only a few ways the creative juices can be stimulated. By stretching your imagination, by expanding your horizons, by breaking with conventional approaches to problems, you can become more inventive, solve difficult problems, and initiate and implement exciting new concepts. This will not only be of benefit to your company, but will also give you that great feeling of accomplishment when you see your ideas successfully realized.

Unfortunately the creative juices that flow easily when nurtured are cut off in many people—from childhood on—by the imposition of overanalysis and conformity by teachers, parents, and eventually bosses. Too often creativity is blocked by red-light thinking. "Stop this." "It's against company policy." "We never did it that way." Instead of looking for reasons not to try new ideas, look at new ideas with an open mind. Turn on the green light. Explore ideas further. Expand your thinking beyond the obvious.

Not every idea is necessarily going to work or is even worth pursuing. However, by at least thinking about it and talking to others about it, you can explore its viability. If it should be rejected, learn the reasons. Don't lose heart. Often the idea, as good as it appears, does not fit the specific application or isn't appropriate at that time. This does not mean it isn't good. It also should not be interpreted as a personal affront. It was the idea that was rejected—not you.

Creativity Can Revive a Dying Enterprise

There are countless examples of companies that were on the verge of failure and were not just saved, but soared ahead thanks to the creative thinking of their leaders.

For more than forty years Pitney Bowes controlled 100 percent of the metered mail market. Nearly half of all mail in the United States passed through the company's machines. But this all stopped when the U.S. Postal Service terminated its monopoly. Competitors with innovative ideas took over and decimated PB's market share.

Fortunately, a leader named Fred Allen stepped in as CEO and visualized Pitney Bowes in a broader light. He posited that PB should not see itself as a postage meter company, but as a company that provides the technology and services for messaging in general. Allen saw that it was the time of faxes and copiers, products that could profit from the company's expertise as well as its reputation for sales and service. The new vision worked, and by the late 1980s fully half of PB's revenues were derived from products introduced only three years before or less. Fred Allen's implementation of his creative vision succeeded in developing a new marketing strategy, as well as the up-to-the-minute office products needed by the new business model.

Other great companies have remained great by boldly reevaluating, reenvisioning, realigning, and redirecting their marketing strategies. The grocery chain Kroger revamped its entire system to create superstores, resulting in the chain's outselling its leading competitors. Abbott, the drug giant, beat out competition in the pharmaceutical industry by concentrating on diagnostics and hospital nutritional products.

To realize their success these businesses often had to overcome resistance from directors and other executives. Fred Allen never lost hope. He had faith that his imagination and creativity and his boldness in implementing his concepts would achieve miraculous results.

When in doubt, remember the achievements of leaders like Fred Allen. Enthrone now in your mind the mental images, ideas, and thoughts that heal, bless, prosper, inspire, and strengthen you. It is true that you become what you imagine yourself to be. Your sustained imagination is sufficient to remake your world. Trust the laws of your mind to bring your good to pass, and you will experience all the blessings and riches of life.

SUM AND SUBSTANCE

- Everybody can be creative. You need not be an Edison or a Bill Gates to be an innovator. You have within you the capacity to stretch your imagination. It is up to you to develop it.

- Through your faculty to imagine the end result, you have control over any circumstance or condition. If you wish to bring about the realization of any wish, desire, idea, or plan, form a mental picture of its fulfillment in your mind. Constantly imagine the reality of your desire. In this way it will infiltrate your subconscious mind and you will actually compel it into being.

- Your imagination can clothe and objectify any idea or desire. You can imagine abundance where lack is, effectiveness where inefficiency is, and growth where stagnation has stymied it.

- Observe what other companies have done when faced with related situations. By adapting approaches that have worked for them, you may be able to deal effectively with your problem.

- Use your imaginative faculties. Seek areas in your job or your business that could be improved. Don't fear trying new approaches. You may have setbacks, but by honing your creative powers, you can succeed in all of your endeavors.

Chapter Ten

Breaking Bad Habits

No matter what bad habits you may have formed or what weaknesses you wish to overcome, you will find the remedy for it within yourself. Whether the habit be a vicious one or some foolish little thing that hinders you in some way, you can get rid of it; you can turn your weaknesses into strength; you can conquer all the enemies of your success and happiness by bringing your divinity, the sublime power that is latent in the great within you, to your aid.

All people are creatures of habit. We tend to do certain things in a certain way whenever we are faced by them. A "habit" can be defined as an "addiction," "custom," "mannerism," or "nature." Some habits or rituals are quite useful. They establish a tradition or routine, thereby providing a measure of order, efficiency, and meaning to a life. Alas, some habits can also lock you into inflexible mindbody patterns and inhibit your openness to change. Habits are a way of life—patterns we follow because we are accustomed to following them. Some habits are good; others bad. The habits we develop in performing our jobs often spell the difference between mediocrity and excellent performance. In this chapter we will examine how habits are developed and how we can overcome bad habits, replace them with good habits, and generally build up patterns of behavior that will lead us to success.

Building Good Habits

The dominant, creative, positive character becomes so by the constant repetition of positive acts and creative thoughts, until such brain processes have become habitual. We may build up a forceful or a weak character, according to our habit of thought. If we hold a self-confident, self-assertive, decisive mental attitude, we will become strong and creative; if we harbor the doubtful, the hesitating, the uncertain, the distrustful, the self-effacing, self-depreciating, self-denunciating thought, we will become negative and ineffectual. It is just a question of which way you set your brain by habitual thinking.

We hear a great deal about luck and circumstances effecting our success or lack of it in our careers. Sure, they may play some part, but more often it is the habits we develop and apply that determine the direction we take. We do not have to choose to go in the wrong direction. All we have to do is follow our inclination, our passion, our normal appetites, our mental inertia, and habit will do the rest. Habit never rests, awake or asleep; it is constantly winding its invisible cords about our thoughts, our character. Whether it is for our weal or our woe, habit is gradually taking charge of us. What we do voluntarily today we shall do more easily tomorrow, and with greater facility the next day.

The best way to develop good habits is, instead of trying to root out a defect or a vicious quality directly, cultivate the opposite quality. Persist in this, and the other will gradually die. Kill the negative by cultivating the positive.

The craving for something higher and better is the best possible antidote or remedy for the lower tendencies which one wishes to get rid of. When the general habit of always aspiring, moving upward and climbing to something higher and better is formed, the undesirable qualities and habits will fade away; they will die from lack of nourishment.

Breaking Bad Habits

It is not an easy matter to overcome a habit of long standing. But the fact that it can be done—at any age—has been proved by thousands of men and women who conquered habits that had almost destroyed their careers and may even have wrecked their lives.

The problem with most people in trying to break away from bad habits or to create good ones is that they do not realize their latent strength and do not make a loud enough call upon their higher, more potent selves. They do not half exert the power of their subconscious mind, the great lever that God has given us to enable us to lift ourselves up to a godlike state. Their resolutions are weak, wishy-washy. They do not put vim enough, grit enough, into them.

One excellent way to kill a bad habit is to strangle it by cutting off the food that nourished it. Don't handle a bad habit tenderly, or try to break it off little by little. Make your attack on the enemy boldly and confidently. Follow the method suggested by Professor William James to free ourselves from the power of an old habit and to form a new one.

"We must take care," he said, "to wrench ourselves from the old habit by as strong and decided initiative as possible. We must accumulate all the possible circumstances that shall reinforce the right motive. We must put ourselves assiduously in positions that encourage the new way. We must make engagements incompatible with the old. We must develop our resolution with every aid we know."

The only way to quit is to quit and to firmly resolve that you will have nothing to do with the thing that is hurting you. If you seriously commit yourself to your resolution and burn your bridges behind you, this very commitment will call to your aid mighty hidden resources of whose very existence you were, perhaps, ignorant. But as long as you leave open a way of retreat, and think that perhaps when the temptation of the old habit becomes too strong you will indulge just a little, you weaken your chances of mastery.

This is not easy to do on the job, where many of the "bad habits" have been ingrained in the way you deal with problems. Often you have used techniques successfully so often that you assume they will always work. They become your "habitual" way of doing the job. But circumstances change and what worked in the past no longer is as effective. Many people stubbornly stick to their habits. "It will work because it always has worked." Smart people recognize and accept that the habitual approach is not the best way of dealing with the problem, break away from the old habit, and seek new approaches.

When a longtime professor of Business Administration was retained by a national retail chain store firm to set up and administer a training program for store managers, he planned training sessions using the same techniques he had been successful using at the university. It didn't take him long to realize that he just wasn't getting through to the trainees.

After a few sessions, the professor and the company's training director discussed his lack of progress. The training director said, "These men and women are active people and are easily bored by lectures."

"But," the professor responded, "lecturing is the way I teach. It's the only way to cover all the material they need to know in the allotted time. It's always worked well. They will get used to it."

The training director disagreed. "You have to involve them more in the process. The teaching style used in college will not work here."

The professor thought long and hard about this. He had developed what he considered an interesting, sometimes even entertaining, lecture style on which he had been frequently complimented. To change his style was like breaking a habit with which he was very comfortable. He resolved to try a new approach. He would hold back, even though he knew it would be hard to resist lecturing, and make the class more participative.

The subject of the next session was the hiring process. Instead of giving the lecture he had prepared, he started by asking the store managers what problems they faced in attracting and selecting new employees. One after another, the trainees told about their methods, their successes and failures, and their concerns in this area. The professor was tempted to give long academic responses, but he remembered his resolution to let the trainees become involved. To his great delight, one manager after another told of his or her experiences, often helping other managers by sharing successes and cautioning about problems that arose. The professor supplemented their stories with brief comments and recaps. By the end of the session, much of what he had intended to lecture on had been covered in the discussion and the class left excited and looking forward to the next session.

The professor reported to the training director that it was the hardest thing he had ever had to do—to keep from dominating the class with his own ideas, but because he did it, both he and the trainees had a successful and rewarding meeting.

Procrastination

One of the most common bad habits that occur in the workplace is procrastination.

"'Tomorrow, tomorrow, not today,' all the lazy people say."

You don't have to be lazy to procrastinate. Most people procrastinate. We tend to put off until the last possible minute things we do not like to do or things we are afraid to do. There are many reasons we procrastinate. We may not like what we have to do, we may prefer to do a different task—but often we procrastinate because we are afraid we will fail.

Everywhere we see splendid ability tied up and compelled to do mediocre work because of the suppressing, discouraging influence of fear. On every hand there are competent people whose efforts are nullified and whose ability to achieve is practically ruined by the development of this monster, which will in time make the most decided person irresolute, the ablest timid and inefficient.

There is no moment like the present. There is no moment at all, no instant force and energy, but in the present. The energy wasted in postponing today's duties until tomorrow would often do the work. How much harder and disagreeable, too, it is to do work that has been put off. Work that could have been done at the time with pleasure or keen enthusiasm becomes drudgery after it has been delayed for days or weeks.

Promptness takes the drudgery out of an occupation. Putting off usually means leaving off, and going to do becomes going undone. Doing a deed is like sowing a seed; if it is not done at just the right time, it will be forever out of season. The summer of eternity will not be long enough to bring to maturity the fruit of a delayed action.

People who always act promptly, even if they make occasional mistakes, will succeed when procrastinators, even if they have the better judgment, will fail.

Here are some suggestions for overcoming procrastination:

- Procrastination is not just failing to meet deadlines—it is failing to get started. So get going! Remember Ben Franklin's adage: "Don't put off until tomorrow what can be done today."

- Put aside the fear of doing something new or different. Delve into the subject and take action.

- When faced with a complex project, don't let it overwhelm you. Break it into manageable components. Set a time schedule for each component.

- Do the things you fear most or dislike most when you are freshest and most energetic.

- Build in interim completion points. Motivating yourself to begin a project that won't come to fruition until a long time in the future can be difficult. By setting interim completion dates for each stage of the project, you get the sense of gratification seeing progress made as you go along.

- Make an arbitrary start. If you don't know how to begin a difficult project, rather than keep mulling it over, make a preliminary assumption and start working. The work itself will stimulate your brain. If it doesn't work out, you can start again. It is better to take an active role than to keep stalling on beginning the project.

- When working on a special project that is over and above the regular work you do, it is tempting to put it off "until I have some free time." Set aside a special time each day to work on it.

- Give yourself a reward when you have completed a task on time that you have usually put off doing.

Acknowledge Your Weaknesses

If you have some vicious habit keeping you back, impeding success on your job, you will be greatly strengthened in your power to overcome it by constantly saying to yourself, "I know this thing (calling it by name) is holding me back. I am not as efficient as I should be; I do not think as clearly, I cannot control my mind so well as I could were I not hampered by this weakness.

"I despise those habits which will keep me back and which will tend to make me a failure. I know that unless I change this habit, it will bind me more strongly to it, and make my chance of breaking away so much less."

Just talk to yourself in this way whenever you are alone and you will be surprised to see how quickly the audible suggestion will weaken the grip of this habit. In a short time your self-talks will so strengthen your commitment that you will be able to entirely eradicate your weakness.

Wally L. was one of those bosses who felt he had to be in total control of his department. He supervised twelve technicians, whose work, although they were proficient, Wally checked and rechecked after—and often during—each assignment. Because turnover in his department was well above that of other units, his boss called him in to discuss this.

"Wally, our exit interviews brought out that the people leaving your department all had the same complaint. They resented you micromanaging their work. You hire good people. You have to let them do their jobs."

"But," Wally replied, "I am responsible for the work of my department. If I don't keep on top of them, I'm not doing my job."

"Wally, good people must be allowed to do their work without somebody looking over their shoulders all the time. I am responsible for your work, but I'm not watching every move you make, because I trust you. You have to trust the people who work for you."

"But if I let them alone, I won't catch errors in time to correct them or maybe not at all."

"There are other ways of keeping control without micromanaging. There are proven techniques on how to delegate work effectively. Learn and apply them."

He explained several of the techniques, which are discussed in detail in Chapter 11 of this book.

Wally thought long and hard about this. He was afraid to give up his tight control but knew it had to be done.

It was hard for Wally to keep from micromanaging his people. When temptation to look over the technician's shoulder came, he said to himself, "Don't do it. You have to trust him."

In time, he built up the trust he needed in each worker and

recognized that although errors occurred from time to time, they were easily detected by the technician at checkpoints and corrected. Work became easier for Wally and the tension in his department lessened. Turnover ceased and Wally had time to expand the work he could do.

Emily R. was always in a rush. Even as a schoolgirl, she hurried through her class work and home assignments, anxious to finish them and get out and play. When she obtained her first job as a data entry clerk, she took the same approach. She was always the first to finish an assignment, but it was frequently filled with errors and had to be redone. Her supervisor cautioned her to slow down and be more careful, but her old school-time practice could not be broken. After a while her boss put her on probation. She said, "Emily, you are a bright person, but your habit of putting speed ahead of accuracy will keep you from ever doing good work. You must break that habit. If you do not improve, we will have to let you go." She suggested that in her next assignment, Emily concentrate on accuracy and not think at all about the time.

Emily was shaken up. She liked the job, but prided herself on her speed. She resolved to try to break that habit. On the next assignment she slowed down for a while, but after a short time began to speed up again. She stopped suddenly, checked the work she had completed, and noted that the first part was totally accurate, but there were several errors in the next part, where she had gone faster. She corrected the errors and continued the work.

She said to herself, "The bad habit is placing me at a great disadvantage in my job; it is holding me up to ridicule, to unfavorable comparison with others. I know that I have more ability than many of those about me who are accomplishing a great deal more. Now I am going to conquer this thing that is destroying my prospects. I am going to get freedom from this urge to put speed before accuracy, no matter how hard it may be."

It took Emily several weeks to finally program her subconscious mind to accept her resolution to minimize speed and concentrate on accuracy, resulting in her becoming one of the top producers in her department.

Don't Dodge the Truth

Acknowledge your bad habits. Do not dodge the issue. You cannot overcome a bad habit if you refuse to admit it.

You are living in a psychological prison of your own making. You are bound by your beliefs, opinions, training, and environmental influences. Like most people, you are a creature of habit. You are conditioned to react the way you do.

You can ingrain the idea of improving your work habits into your mentality so that it reaches your subconscious depths. At that point, you will achieve a new understanding of how your mind works. You will discover within yourself the infinite resources to back up your statement and prove the truth to yourself.

If you have a keen desire to free yourself from these detriments to your capabilities, you are already 51 percent healed. When your desire to give up the bad habit is greater than your need to continue it, you will be amazed to discover that overcoming it is but a step away.

Whatever thought you anchor the mind upon, the mind magnifies. Engage the mind on the concept of success and achievement. Keep it focused on this new direction of attention. In doing so, you generate feelings that gradually pervade the concept of success and achievement. Whatever idea you emotionalize in this way is accepted by your subconscious and brought to pass.

SUM AND SUBSTANCE

It is never easy to break bad habits, but it can be done. Here are ten suggestions that should help you to free yourself from patterns of behavior that have kept you from being the man or woman you truly want to be:

1. *Choose the habit you wish to change.* Target a habit that is not only a disturbing element in your life, but one which holds you back from achieving your goals. Select a self-defeating pattern which you can focus your discontent on and turn around constructively.

2. *Assess the problem.* After choosing a target habit, identify what you actually do and what you really want to do. Break a big problem into manageable bite-size pieces.

3. *Establish a challenging and achievable goal and time frame.* The goals should be challenging yet obtainable; if you properly and gradually stretch your horizons and actions, you should reach your desired objectives.

4. *Prepare to grieve the loss of the habit.* Both before you start and/or during your habit-changing program, don't be surprised if you experience a poignant, if not profound, sense of loss. You may miss the satisfaction of finding mistakes when you micromanage or the high you may get by finishing a project first—even if not most accurately. But in time your subconscious mind will adjust and you will no longer feel that loss.

5. *Consult with a coach or counselor.* Seek the experience and wisdom of a friend or mentor or a professional counselor to act as your coach in this start-up phase. He or she will help you set goals, provide tips and support for managing the uncomfortable emotions that are likely to surface, and give you suggestions and encouragement when you fall behind.

6. *Take action.* Do it! Take the first step. You'll quickly get feedback regarding what you can and can't handle, along with available resources. You'll definitely glean insight regarding vital survival knowledge, skills, and critical supports.

7. *Join with groups of others* who wish to break the same bad habit or develop a new habit. When several people with the same goal interact, there is an added dimension to the support each gives the other members of the group. Look into such groups as Alcoholics Anonymous, geared to help with specific situations.

8. *Do it systematically.* Behavior modification is an evolutionary process; it often comes in three distinct phases: (1) freeing yourself from the old pattern, (2) making the change, and (3) mastering the new pattern. The first phase involves acknowledging the self-defeating patterns and starting to let go. The second phase tries to incorporate new skills, tools, resources, and positive activities. If the first step is depressing, the middle phase can be anxiety provoking, as you awkwardly apply new insights. The final phase occurs when trial and error, along with practice, lead to the mastery of the new habit. The change starts feeling more natural.

9. *Don't give up!* One of the seductive traps about behavior modification is that sometimes there is rapid learning at the beginning of the process. And then you hit a plateau. Don't give up. Don't get overly optimistic after quick victories or too deflated with some setbacks. It's nature's way to ebb and flow . . . and to get knocked down and then get up and moving again.

   Success is getting up one more time than we fall down; being courageous one more time than we are fearful; being trusting one more time than we are anxious.

10. *Pursue the path.* Pursuing the path you take, overcoming hurdles and obstacles along the way, is an integral part of the learning process. Breaking, making, and mastering a deep-seated, intricate behavior-learning chain is a lifetime process.

PART TWO

Obtaining Cooperation and Support of Others

Do not think ill of another for to do so is to administer poison to yourself. Love is the answer to getting along with others. Love is respecting the divinity of the other.

Your success in your career often depends on other people. They may be people within your organization, such as your bosses, your subordinates, and your colleagues. Sometimes they may be outside of your organization, such as customers or clients.

You will have to motivate members of your staff, your managers, even your customers and suppliers, to work with you to reach established goals. To do this you will have to sharpen your communication skills and your ability to persuade others to accept your ideas. You will have to learn how to deal with difficult people, how to disagree without being disagreeable, how to make the most of your time, and in general how to become an effective leader.

In the following chapters you will learn how to achieve all of this by maximizing the power of your subconscious mind to obtain the cooperation and collaboration of those men and women with whom you interact on the road to success.

Chapter Eleven

Becoming a Leader

You will never succeed in leadership unless you truly believe you can be a leader. You must instill in your subconscious mind two simple conditions: You must believe that what you want can happen. You must believe that it will happen.

All successful people are not leaders. But all good leaders are successful people. Not only are they personal achievers, but they also inspire others to be achievers. They do not only enjoy the fruits of their success, but also strive to help others become successful.

The belief that leaders are born—not made—has been generally accepted throughout the ages. Indeed, it was the basis of feudalism and the system of absolute monarchy. Even in America, where people of humble beginnings have risen to high positions, many still feel that they were born with the traits that made them leaders.

In most business organizations certain men and women rise from the ranks to positions of supervision and management. Are all of these people "natural leaders"? Experience has shown that the answer is "Not necessarily."

People move into positions of leadership and responsibility for many reasons: seniority, election (in the public sector), nepotism, or superior performance. They are not chosen for their leadership ability or experience, so they have to be taught to be leaders. The achievement of a higher position does not ensure success in leadership. People have to learn to lead. They study leadership techniques and read inspiring books, attend lectures and put into practice what they have learned.

Characteristics of Great Leaders

Although each of the great leaders of the past and present have special characteristics that make them great, there are some aspects of their personalities that they all have in common. In my opinion, outstanding leaders all share the following qualities:

1. *Great leaders identify, cultivate, and inspire enthusiastic followers.* Few businesses or enterprises can survive and thrive without staffs of people to carry out the leader's programs. In every generation, in every country, in every aspect of life, it has been such people who have led armies to victories, inspired great art and music, and developed prosperous companies and dynamic organizations. The art of all arts for the leader is the ability to measure others, weigh them, to "size them up," to estimate their strength and eliminate their weakness.

Leaders surround themselves with people who have the ability that they lack, who can supplement their weakness and shortcomings with strength and ability. Thus, in their combined power, they make an effective force. To do this a good leader may often have to shake up his organization and even step aside.

A good example of this is Sean Perich, founder of Bakery Barn, producer of a protein cookie. He grew the company to the $6 million level in fewer than five years, through sales at fitness gyms and 7-Elevens. But somewhere around 2005, Bakery Barn's rise to the top stalled, forcing Perich to look again at his team, himself included. The company had veered off into new products based on his own ideas, which went unquestioned. His senior management team (primarily family members) had been fine at the beginning, but now he recognized that neither he nor they had the culinary or business experience needed to save the company. Fresh blood was needed. So he hired a full-time comptroller and started interviewing presidential candidates. He also got a three-person research and development team to bring new and more objective insights into management decisions.

This bold, difficult move was also required of a much more high-profile founder, David Neeleman, once CEO of JetBlue, an innovative "no-frills" airline. Though he remained on as chairman of the board, Neeleman realized that he did not have the managerial skills to take JetBlue to the next level. That didn't mean he wasn't a great visionary and entrepreneur. On the contrary, what it proved was that he was all that and more: a true leader.

2. *Great leaders focus their efforts.* Great leaders know what they want and concentrate their efforts to reach those goals. The people who do not learn to focus their efforts early in life, to centralize power, will never achieve marked success in anything. People who have the power of unification, whose every effort has reference to one central aim, are the ones who reach the top of the wall. They understand that it is not the amount of work than can be accomplished at a stretch, but rather persistence that tells. It is the long, steady pull, the unconquerable purpose, and the unbroken effort that win the battle of life.

3. *Great leaders have faced and overcome great difficulties.* Adversity can destroy some people, but all good leaders have faced adversity and bounced back to greater glories. Robert Fulton, the creator of the steamboat, failed several times. His ship was derided as "Fulton's Folly" until finally it made its first successful voyage and revolutionized water transportation. Helen Keller, blind and deaf since infancy, overcame this handicap and became a respected and idolized writer and educator.

A shy, unpretentious in-house lawyer named Darwin E. Smith became CEO of Kimberly-Clark, then a declining traditional paper manufacturer, in 1971. K-C's stock had fallen badly over the years. At least one director didn't hesitate to remind Smith that he wasn't exactly qualified to lead the company, but that didn't stop the new CEO from utterly transforming Kimberly-Clark, from an uninspired brand to the leading paper-based consumer products company in the world. Smith had grown up poor and used the experience to steel his resolve. Two months after becoming CEO, he was diagnosed with cancer and was told he had a year to live. He used his predicament to call up some more resolve. He programmed his subconscious mind to believe that he could overcome this disease and pushed out all thoughts and fears of failure. He refused to lie down and die. He continued going to work during his radiation treatment, and not only revitalized his own life but rebuilt his company.

What the business world most admires about the little-known Darwin Smith, though, is one of his first executive decisions: to sell the mills. He and his team had decided that the coated paper end of the business wasn't where Kimberly-Clark should be headed any longer, and that throwing K-C into the hotly competitive consumer paper products industry would force the company to either thrive or die. It was the gutsiest move anyone had ever seen. The business press damned the decision as stupid, and Wall Street downgraded the company's stock. But Smith's resolve held. Twenty-five years later, Smith had the competition solidly beat and is today a leader in the industry. He explained his success by saying that he simply never stopped believing in himself and in the viability of his company.

4. *Great leaders expect more from themselves than they do from others.* Success is not dependent solely on your earnest affirmation, on your self-confidence, but also on the confidence of others in you; but this confidence is very largely a reflection of your own, the effect of your own personality on them. Your own attitude of mind is therefore the means to produce this confidence in others. Your earnest affirmation is contagious. It affects everyone with whom you come in contact, especially those whom you must master, whether as a teacher, an orator, an attorney, a sales rep, a merchant, a possible employee, or in some other way. There is something that seems almost magical in the way a confident air influences other people. If you adopt or acquire it, you will be surprised to see how soon it will radiate to others, increasing their confidence in your ability to do the thing you undertake.

Never lose your self-confidence. If at times you begin to doubt your capabilities and strengths, reread Chapter 2 of this book and reinforce the power of your subconscious mind to rebuild your self-confidence.

5. *Great leaders are not afraid to make tough decisions.* Whether leading a nation or a corporation, every day the leader faces problems that require decisions. In some cases there is adequate time to think, to assess and evaluate all of the circumstances surrounding the problem, but quite often an immediate decision is needed. The good leader must make such decisions.

An outstanding example of this occurred in September 1982, when seven people died after taking Tylenol. It was discovered that several bottles of that product had been tampered with—cyanide, a deadly poison, had been injected into the tablets. McNeil Laboratories, a division of Johnson & Johnson, the manufacturers of Tylenol, took immediate action. They recalled all of the product on the market and destroyed it. More important, the top management of the firm went on TV and explained the situation. They assured the public that Tylenol would not be reintroduced until every caution had been taken to make it safe.

The immediate result was catastrophic. Market share fell from 35 percent to only 8 percent. But because of the rapid and sincere response of the leaders of McNeil and J&J, the market share was not only recovered but exceeded within a year.

Another example of an executive who made a tough and unpopular decision is Charles R. "Cork" Walgreen, who took over the Walgreens drugstore company in 1975. At that time most drugstores had lunch counters, which provided a significant share of their income. Cork Walgreen felt that the growth of the fast-food chains had made the drugstore food operations obsolete and decided that the company's future lay in product sales, not food service. It was a controversial decision, as the company had five hundred lunch counters. The connection to this side of the business was not as much financial as it was emotional. The Walgreens food-service division dated back to Cork's grandfather, so it took a great deal of resolve on the part of Cork Walgreen to put an end to all that. Cork's decision paid off, as Walgreens today is one of the most profitable companies in its field—and lunch counters are virtually gone from all drugstores.

6. *Great leaders have a vision and utmost faith in themselves to fulfill that vision.* The great leaders of the world all have had their visions. They knew what they wanted to accomplish, visualized its outcome, and devoted all their energies and emotions to accomplishing that vision. Most important, they truly believed in their own capability to do this. Having such faith gave them the strength to pursue these goals.

American Express CEO Ken Chenault has been faced with many surprises and detours, but none as dramatic as the one that took place directly across the street from American Express headquarters on September 11, 2001. He refers to that tragedy as a formative experience that added to his already formidable leadership abilities. Chenault saw the obvious on 9/11—that it was a crisis, and would be seen by many as a major obstacle to the progress of his leadership. Chenault did not hesitate to make key decisions. His faith in his ability to lead enabled him to call on his leadership skills. Agreeing that the most valuable experiences always seem to come in the form of crises, Chenault says it's essential at such a time to utilize the attributes that are really important and focus on them so you're not just using them unconsciously, but consciously. This gives a leader an advantage. He says everyone can make the conscious choice to be a leader. The kind of outstanding leaders Chenault says he wants to work with are what he describes as "rationally and emotionally engaged people."

7. *Great leaders are ambitious for themselves, their company, and their people.* No matter how poor you may be, how humble your lot, look up. Don't be afraid to aim too high. Keep your eye fixed upon your star. Let others ridicule, if they will, but do not let them induce you to relax the fixity of your gaze. It is this setting the eye on a single star that has distinguished the great men and women of every age.

Mary Kay Ash, the founder of Mary Kay cosmetics, attributed her success to her lifelong ambition to reach the top. Her sales career began when she joined Stanley Home Products, a door-to-door marketing firm. She often commented that she was not at all successful during her first year and was ready to give up. This changed when she attended her first Stanley sales seminar.

She reported, "There I saw this tall, svelte, pretty, successful woman crowned queen as a reward for being the best in a company contest and I determined to be that queen the following year, which seemed impossible. However, I decided to go up and talk to the president and to tell him that I intended to be queen next year. He didn't laugh at me, but looked me in the eye, held my hand and said: 'Somehow I think you will.' Those five words drove me and the next year I was queen."

Mary Kay started her own business in 1963 in a five-hundred-square-foot storefront in Dallas, with the help of her family, a life savings of $5,000, and only nine sales force members. Over the years under her leadership the company showed continuing growth. By demonstrating her commitment to her own and her company's success, Mary Kay inspired her sales staff to set high goals for themselves and to work hard to attain them. In 2007, there were more than one million independent sales reps in the Mary Kay organization, grossing more than $2,400,000,000 in sales.

Delegation

One of the key requirements for success as a leader is the ability and willingness to delegate decision making to subordinates. Too many managers are reluctant to do this. Successful leaders recognize that they cannot do everything. They hire and train the most capable people they can find and allow them to make decisions within their areas of expertise, so they are free to use their time on matters at a higher level.

Most managers have more work to do than they can ever expect to accomplish in the course of a normal workday. In order to get it done, they must delegate part of that work to subordinates.

To delegate means to assign a subordinate duties or tasks and the power and authority to perform them. It is not just assigning the least challenging or unpleasant parts of the job to subordinates. Effective delegation requires that significant aspects of the work be delegated. This not only frees up the executive to do more important tasks, but also enables the subordinate to gain from the experience.

Business leaders have often told me that they are so accustomed to performing many of the tasks they do—and do it so well—that they are reluctant to delegate the work to others. As one manager told me, "I find myself looking over my people's shoulders as they work. I just don't feel comfortable delegating."

The first step is to acknowledge that even though you can do the job faster and perhaps better than subordinates, your time is much too valuable to waste on lesser matters. Here are some guidelines that will enable you to delegate with confidence:

- *Select capable people.* In choosing your key subordinates, be sure that they are not only capable of doing the work for which you hire them, but have the potential to be trained to move up into positions of higher responsibility.

- *Communicate what you are delegating clearly and concisely.* To ensure that the subordinate understands what you expect from him or her, don't just ask, "Do you understand?" Most people will just say "Yes." Perhaps they really do understand; perhaps they think they understand but their interpretation of what you want is different from yours; or perhaps they don't understand at all but are too embarrassed to tell you. Ask specific questions about what the subordinate plans to do to carry out the assignment.

- *Set control points.* A control point is a place at which you stop, examine what has been accomplished, and if errors have been made—correct them. This is important because if major errors are not discovered until the last minute, the problem will get out of hand. A control point is not a surprise inspection. The subordinate knows exactly when each control point will occur and what should be accomplished by then. Having control points does not mean you do not have confidence in the subordinate. Let your people know at the outset that you do have confidence in them and emphasize that control points are designed to help them—not check them. Control points enable them to measure their progress themselves.

- *Give your subordinates the tools and authority to get the job done.* If the assignment requires expenditure of money, include in the delegation a budget for the work and the authority for the person doing it to spend the allotted amount without asking your approval for each expense. If the work requires hiring additional personnel or having people work overtime, give them the authority for this as part of the delegation. This will ensure that you will not be constantly interrupted in your work to deal with these matters.

- *Provide help if and when needed.* This may sound like a contradiction. You delegate to curtail your own activities in the area delegated. If you offer to help, are you not encouraging interruptions? To minimize the time spent on this, require that when a subordinate brings you a problem, he or she bring with it a suggested solution. In this way the subordinate will have to think about it and quite often will find his or her own solution and not come to you at all. And if the subordinate does come, the time spent on dealing with the problem will be much shorter.

Know Your Strengths and Limitations

Before you can enter the race and be admitted to the success track, you must first of all have a definite purpose, a high, unwavering aim, and you must have the courage, grit, and determination to cling to it no matter what stands in the way or opposes you.

You will never succeed in leadership unless you truly believe you can be a leader. You must instill in your subconscious mind two simple conditions: You must believe that what you want *can* happen. You must believe that it *will* happen.

There is a force in spoken words that is not stirred by going over the same words mentally. When vocalized, words make a more lasting impression upon the mind. Many of us are more powerfully impressed and inspired by listening to a great lecture or sermon than by reading the same thing in print. We remember the spoken word when we forget the cold type that carries thought to the brain. It makes a deeper impression on the inner self.

We can talk to our inner or subconscious mind just as we would talk to a child, and we know from experience that it will listen to and act on our suggestions. We are constantly sending suggestions or commands to our subconscious mind. We may not do so audibly, but we do so silently, mentally. Unconsciously we advise, we suggest, we try to influence it in certain directions.

By consciously, audibly addressing it, in heart-to-heart talks with ourselves, we find that we can very materially influence our habits, our motives, and our methods of living. In fact, the possibilities of influencing the character and the life by this means are practically limitless.

Start by writing out a list of the qualities that make a strong, courageous, successful character, and their opposites, those that make a weak, timid, unsuccessful one, and examine yourself to see what your rating is on each list. Call the characteristics off aloud: faith, courage, self-confidence, ambition, enthusiasm, perseverance, concentration, initiative, cheerfulness, optimism, thoroughness, etc. Ask yourself if you possess these splendid qualities, or if you incline toward their opposites.

Don't be afraid to face your weak points, or to call your faults by their right names. Bring them into the light, see them for what they are, and then grapple with them. You cannot afford to be less than God intended you to be, to be less than you feel that you should be and can be, to have your life spoiled by some defect that you can overcome.

When you have gone over the specific character qualities, ask yourself these broader questions, always visualizing and addressing yourself by name:

"Bob, what are you here for? What do you mean to the world? What message does your life, your career bring to it? What do you mean to your company, organization, or community?"

"Beth, what do you stand for? What do you represent? Are you delivering it patiently, persistently, determinedly, without grumbling, whining, or shirking?"

Ask yourself: "Am I dreaming of the big thing I am going to do tomorrow, or am I just doing the little things that I can do today?"

Probe yourself in this manner until you get a good line on yourself, a fair estimate of yourself, until you know both your strengths and your weaknesses, until you can see with clear eyes the things that are keeping you back, the lack in your nature that is handicapping you. Your weaknesses are cutting down the average of your ability by 10, 20, 50, or even 75 percent. Then vigorously attack your enemies, the enemies of your success, of your efficiency, of your happiness. Constantly, stoutly affirm your complete mastery over them, their powerlessness to dominate your life and ruin your career.

Engage Your Subconscious Mind

By heart-to-heart talks of this sort with yourself you can change your whole nature, and revolutionize your career. Whether it is faith, courage, initiative, cheerfulness—whatever it is you lack, assume the quality you wish to possess, affirm positively that it is already yours, exercise it whenever possible, concentrate on it, and you will be surprised how quickly you can acquire the desired.

We need to tell our subconscious exactly what we want. We need to direct it to help us attain our goals. When you know what your true desire really is, your unconscious mind will propel you unerringly toward it. But it needs to know that you genuinely, fervently, and unwaveringly want this goal, and that you will not forsake it for all the other conflicting and contradictory wishes, notions, and momentary fancies that flit through your mind.

Power comes from within or from nowhere. Be yourself. Listen to the voice within. There is room for improvement in every profession, in every trade, and in every business. The world wants people who can do things in new and better ways. Don't think that because your plan or idea has no precedent, or because you are young and inexperienced, you will not get a hearing. The person who has anything new and valuable to give to the world will be listened to and will be followed. If you have a strong individuality and dare to think your own thoughts and originate your own methods, if you are not afraid to be yourself, and are not a copy of someone else, you will quickly get recognition.

Until you erase "fate" and "can't" and "doubt" from your vocabulary, you cannot rise. You cannot get strong while you harbor convictions of your weakness, or be happy while you dwell on your miseries or misfortunes.

Be Committed to What You Want to Accomplish

One of the most effective ways to motivate yourself is to be firmly committed to what you desire to accomplish. When things go wrong, when obstacles seem unconquerable, when discouragement raises its face, your commitment will motivate you to keep up the fight.

The only way to develop power is to resolve early in life never to let an opportunity for doing so go by. Never shrink from anything that will give you more discipline, better training, and enlarged experience. No matter how distasteful, force yourself into it. There is nothing like responsibility for developing ability. Never mind if the position is hard; take it and make up your mind that you are going to fill it better than it has ever been filled before.

Leaders must blaze their own way, make their own path, or they will never make much of an impression on the world. It is striking originality that attracts attention. To be a leader, do not follow others. Do not imitate. Do not do things just as everybody else has done them before, but try new, ingenious ways. Show the people in your specialty that precedents do not cut much of a figure with you, and that you will make your own program.

Don't be afraid to trust yourself. Have faith in your own ability to think along original lines. Whatever you do, cultivate a spirit of independence in doing it.

SUM AND SUBSTANCE

- You will never succeed in leadership unless you truly believe you can be a leader. You must instill in your subconscious mind two simple conditions: You must believe that what you want *can* happen. You must believe that it *will* happen.

- One of the key requirements for success as a leader is the ability and willingness to delegate decision making to subordinates. Too many managers are reluctant to do this. Successful leaders recognize that they cannot do everything. A successful leader hires and trains the most capable people he or she can find and allows them to make decisions within their areas of expertise, so that the leader is free to use his or her time on matters of a higher level of importance.

- Don't think that because your plan or idea has no precedent, or because you are young and inexperienced, you will not get a hearing. The person who has anything new and valuable to give to the world will be listened to and will be followed.

- Don't be afraid to face your weak points, or to call your faults by their right names. Bring them into the light, see them for what they are, and then grapple with them. You cannot afford to be less than God intended you to be, to be less than you feel that you should be and can be, to have your life spoiled by some defect that you can overcome.

- To be a leader, do not follow others. Do not imitate. Do not do things just as everybody else has done them before, but try new, ingenious ways. Show the people in your specialty that precedents do not cut much of a figure with you, and that you will make your own program.

Chapter Twelve

Creating a Dynamic Team

Wish for others what you wish for yourself. This is the key to harmonious human relations.

The working world has changed radically during the past decade, and it continues to change more rapidly than at any time since the Industrial Revolution. Things are likely to change even more dramatically over the next several decades.

It used to be that top management made all the decisions and filtered them down through a series of layers to the rank-and-file workers. We have seen and continue to see this being replaced by a more collaborative organization in which people at all levels are expected to contribute to every aspect of their organization's activities. Getting things done is now assumed by teams—groups of people, usually headed by a team leader, who together plan, implement, and control the work.

The essence of a team is common commitment. Without this commitment, the members of the group perform as individuals; with it, they become a powerful unit of collective performance.

In the ideal team, each associate performs his or her function in such a way that dovetails with that of other team members to enable the team to achieve its goals. By this collaboration, the whole becomes greater than the sum of its parts.

An excellent example of this is a surgical team. Every member of the team—the surgeon, the anesthesiologist, the nurses, and the other technicians—carries out his or her individual functions expertly. In a skillfully functioning surgical team, a seamless flow of interactions occurs among the members. All are committed to one goal—the well-being of the patient.

There are examples of successful teams in every endeavor: championship sports, disease-curing research, firefighting and rescue, and in every aspect of business.

Managing Your Team

If your philosophy of managing people is "Do it my way or you're on the highway," you'd better prepare to make an about-face. The team leader does not function like that old-school tyrant. He or she is a facilitator who develops and coordinates an intelligent, motivated team to gets things done. The emphasis is on developing the skills and coordinating the efforts of a team of intelligent, motivated associates.

Don't Boss—Lead

To create a dynamic, motivated team, you have to stop thinking like a "boss." Bosses make decisions and give orders. Team leaders coordinate groups of thinking adults who together face and work out the problems they encounter. Successful team leaders provide a climate in which their team members are encouraged to make their own analyses of problems, suggest solutions, and participate in decisions. Let's look at some of the ways team leaders do this:

- They make sure the team members know the organization's and the team's vision and mission, and keep them focused on achieving them.

- They're expert communicators and recognize that communication is a two-way street. It is important for leaders to convey their instructions and concepts to team members, but it is equally important for them to open their ears to team members' ideas and suggestions.

- They aim to develop their team members' skills and capabilities. Successful leaders take the time to identify each team member's strengths and weaknesses and work with each member to improve his or her performance. They encourage team members to commit to lifelong learning and recommend sources—both within and outside the organization—that can help them grow as individuals and as team contributors.

- They work with members to set performance standards that are clear, attainable, and measurable, and establish a means to let members know how they are doing.

- They motivate and inspire individual team members through recognition, praise, and reward. They motivate and inspire the team with pep talks, team recognition, and by creating a climate of enthusiasm.

Apply "the Golden Rule"

"Do unto others as you would have others do unto you." The Golden Rule appears in some form in all the world's great religions. It is often called the essence of religion. When asked to boil the Scriptures down to one major teaching, the great Jewish scholar Hillel, who lived a century before Jesus, responded: "The most important idea is not to do to your fellow man what you would not want him to do to you." Modern psychologists reiterate this rule as the prime factor in the development of sound interpersonal relations.

What does following the Golden Rule have to do with becoming a successful team leader? Hillel also answers this question. He said: "If I am not for myself, who will be for me? But if I am only for myself, what am I?" Yes, God gave us the power to have wealth and abundance. It is our obligation to make the most of our own talents and opportunities, but with it comes the obligation to look out not just for ourselves but also for others.

You will find the Golden Rule principle woven like a golden thread into all major systems of philosophy and worship. It may not appear in the same words, but the intent of the idea is identical: that we should *give* to others, allow and desire for others, the same freedoms of belief, worship, achievement, and acquisition that we desire for ourselves.

When we adopt this attitude as our ethical code—our guiding principle—it becomes a dynamic influence and energy in our daily lives. It is the treasure of wisdom within the depths of our being—a guide, an inner directive from the heart and soul of every man and woman.

We must program our subconscious minds to accept that we are not just for ourselves but part of the team, and each teammate is a partner, a person, who assumes and accepts responsibility for the team's success and is willing to contribute a fair share of effort and attitude toward ensuring it.

When we allow others perfect freedom to think, speak, and make decisions with all their minds and hearts—we are deeming them as we deem ourselves. It is a partnership in which we are giving at least as much as we expect to receive.

What It Takes to Be a Great Team Member

As mentioned earlier, a team leader is not the boss of the team but the first among equals. All team members must work together to achieve the team's goals. Succeeding as a team member starts by performing your job superbly. All team members are depended upon to be good performers. But top performance by itself is not enough. There's a great deal more to becoming a great team member. Here are some guidelines to help achieve this goal:

- *Participate fully in team discussions and listen actively.* Contribute to every discussion. Even if you have no original ideas to present, comment on other members' suggestions and ask good questions. Offer your support. Volunteer to help.

- *Motivate yourself.* Set personal goals that are in line with your team's mission. Participate in establishing team goals. You are going to have to work to meet them, so you should have a say in determining them.

- *Try new things.* Don't be afraid to take risks. This is the way to get ahead. Remember the turtle. It's perfectly secure if it stays inside the shell, but if it wants to move ahead, it has to stick out its neck.

- *Look beyond your team.* Study the culture of your organization. Know and understand its mission statement. Measure how closely your team complies with organizational and departmental goals. Think about how your work fits into the larger picture.

- *Be sensitive to other points of view.* Listen to the opinions of other team members. Don't be afraid to express your view even if it is different from or even the opposite of everybody else's. Stand up for what you believe, but don't be stubborn about it. Be willing to compromise to achieve consensus.

- *Be a team player*. Cooperate. Don't compete. Support your teammates. Help them grow by sharing information, taking tough assignments, and training and mentoring new members. Praise associates who have done well. Show appreciation to members who have been especially helpful to you or the team.

- *Know your teammates*. Know their strengths and limitations. Know their personal goals and ambitions. Know their idiosyncrasies and pet peeves. This will make working with them easier and more pleasant.

- *Build up your own self-confidence*. Reread Chapter 2 of this book and apply what you have learned. In addition, read self-improvement books and articles. Study yourself. Be aware of areas where you need improvement. For example, if you are shy, take assertiveness training; if you are a poor speaker or writer, take courses to correct it.

- *Don't let conflicts stifle your team's progress*. If you and a teammate have a disagreement or more serious conflict, resolve it as rapidly as possible. Don't let it fester. Once it is resolved, forget about it. Don't bear a grudge. "Let the dead past bury its dead."

- *Learn other jobs within the team*. Train to do the work of other team members. In this way you expand your value to the team, as you can take over in case of absence, heavy workloads, or other contingencies.

- *Keep tabs on your progress*. Periodically review your personal and team goals. Measure how close you are to reaching them. Be prepared to take steps to correct problems that are impeding your progress.

The concept of the team is based on the principle that its members all work together to achieve the desired results. This means that all team members do whatever has to be done to accomplish the job. This includes doing work you don't enjoy, helping slower members catch up, and putting aside pet projects to keep the team on target for higher priority assignments.

The Importance of Trust

The basis for any relationship, on or off the job, is trust. If team members do not trust their leader or one or more of their teammates, the team will never get off the ground.

The success or failure of a team leader depends on the trust of his or her team. If people trust you, anything you say can be heard. If people don't trust you, then most of what you say will go in one ear and out the other.

It doesn't take much for a person to lose trust in another. The team leader makes a promise and then fails to live up to it. Trust is lost. A member withholds needed information from other members; nobody trusts that member again.

Rebuilding trust is not easy. If the lack of trust is among team members, the team leader can step in to alleviate the problem. However, if the team leader has lost the trust of the team members, it will take extraordinary effort to reestablish a trusting relationship.

Men and women who are deemed worthy of being your collaborators must trust themselves, have faith in their own ability to think along original lines. If there is any potential in them, self-reliance will bring it out.

Whatever you do, encourage your team members to cultivate a spirit of independence in carrying out their plans. Give them the opportunity to express themselves in their work. Instead of being a mere cog in a machine, encourage them to do their own thinking and carry out their own ideas, as far as possible, even though working for another.

Change Is Not Easy

Changing the way you work is often not easy. It requires a radical change in the way you look at your job—and at yourself. Nobody really likes to change the way they do things. You're accustomed to doing your job in a certain way. It's comfortable to keep doing it that way. Changing takes you out of this comfort zone. But progress can't be made unless you become uncomfortable. You have to delve deep into your subconscious mind and cleanse it of old habits and build into it the new ways of doing things.

It's a difficult procedure, but it is well worth it. Some of the benefits you gain are:

1. *Your job.* It's as simple as that. If the company goes down the drain, you have no job. If the company prospers, not only do you have a job, but the opportunities within the firm expand. In today's highly competitive world, if a company is to thrive—even survive—it must change. But no company can change unless all of its members contribute to that change. By accepting change, you are doing a small part in keeping your company viable. By enthusiastically supporting change, you are increasing your company's capability to meet the competition.

2. *Your personal growth.* The team environment challenges its members to use their intelligence, their creativity, and their skills in working on team problems. Now, often for the first time on your job you can express your ideas and contribute to the way a job is done. This stimulates your mind, and encourages you to build up your knowledge. With each success, your self-confidence increases. When there are setbacks—and there will be—focusing on past successes instead of fretting about the current situation helps you develop the resilience you need to accept and learn from the setback.

3. *Your career.* If your goal is to move up the organizational ladder, active participation in team activities will give you needed experience in leadership. You'll take part in running meetings, leading projects, and training and mentoring associates. You'll catch the eye of higher level managers as your contributions are recognized. When new teams are formed, you will be prepared to be moved into team leadership.

Overcoming Resistance to Change

It is not only you who may be resistant to change; others in your organization may also fight any effort to shift from work groups to teams. Most people resist change and will find any excuse to keep things the way they are.

Often, when faced with changes in the way work is performed, people react with "But we've always done it this way." To make changes in the way work is done, team members have to be sold on the benefits of the changes.

Another reason people may give for keeping things the way they are is "If it ain't broke, don't fix it," or its companion comment, "Don't mess with success."

There's no question that many of the processes, procedures, and methods with which work has been done have been successful. Change should not be made just for the sake of change. The point is that even if the process "ain't broke" and works fine, it should be looked at to see what changes might be made so it will be even more effective when converted to a team activity.

There's no way the changeover to teams will work unless top executives in the organization are convinced of its value and give it full support.

First-line supervisors may fear that their roles will be diminished and perhaps their jobs abolished, and look at their changing role as a diminution of their status.

Changing from supervisor to team leader is not accomplished

overnight. It takes time and is sometimes difficult. Supervisors must be clearly shown how they would benefit from the change. They must be assured that by delegating some of their functions, they will give themselves more time to improve overall processes, tackle new projects, and broaden the scope of their jobs. If you feed their conscious minds with this assurance, their subconscious minds will absorb and adjust, and aid them in accepting needed changes.

Make Job Design a Team Effort

A team consists of members who possess a variety of skills that can be unified to achieve the team's objectives. Who does what should be clear and consistent with the direction of the team. All members should know where they fit into the overall picture and how, by working together, they will accomplish much more than they could as individuals.

In designing the jobs that the team will perform, the team leader should take advantage of the know-how and experience of all of the members. Just as team goals are more effective when determined by the entire team, so is the design of the job—the processes and methods used to carry out the goals.

Collaboration on the Job

The old saying that "two minds are better than one" can be expanded to "three minds are better than two," and so on. If we can utilize the brainpower of others combined with our own, the possibilities for success are enhanced.

By working in close collaboration with team members and with specialists in areas outside of your own expertise, not only do you learn from them (and they from you), but also the interaction within the group acts as a stimulant to your own thinking. It hones your intelligence; it sharpens your perspective; it stimulates your creativity. It enhances the power of your subconscious mind to enable you to make more innovative and wiser decisions.

Quite often, ideas from one person spark ideas in others. Within your brain is the potential for creating unlimited thoughts. Much of our brainpower lies deep in our subconscious. It's just waiting to be uncovered. When a group of people discuss a situation, ideas are brought up from the subconscious of one team member by something one of the other team members says. Any idea can plant a seed in another's mind that sprouts into another idea; as each person expresses thoughts and concepts, each of the other participants absorbs, adapts, and shapes those ideas in his or her own mind, and the collaborative effort results in new thinking that could not have occurred by itself.

Collaboration Enhances Enthusiasm

When people participate in making a decision, they commit themselves to its success. The fact that they have been part of the decision-making process gives them "ownership" of the program. And there is nothing as powerful as ownership to generate enthusiasm. The mind keeps repeating: "It's my project. It has to succeed."

What goes on in the mind is what determines outcome. When people really get enthusiastic, you can see it in the flash of their eyes, in their alert and vibrant personality. You can observe it in the spring of their step. You can see it in the verve of their whole being. Enthusiasm makes the difference in one's attitude toward other people, toward one's job, toward the world. It makes the big difference in the zest and delight of human existence.

Michelle Peluso, CEO of Travelocity, the highly successful online travel service, ensures she has enthusiastic teams to back her up, by making sure they remain engaged. Her philosophy is that people go to work because they believe in the people around them and what they all stand for: their peers, their colleagues, and their conviction that their company does something great for its customers.

Peluso engages her staff in various ways: She sends weekly emails describing how Travelocity is championing the customer experience. She asks employees to nominate a colleague who reflects the company's core values, and she features them and descriptions of their work. She encourages team members to make a practice of regular communication with the team—not just to deal with a problem. She relates directly with all of her teams by holding monthly brown bag lunches anyone can attend, and she makes herself available for casual, open conversations. She makes quarterly visits to offices and openly discusses the company's finances, competitive position, and other matters, which is impressive to team members who like to know their efforts are getting results.

Develop Your Teammates by Giving Them Responsibility

Responsibility is a great power developer. Where there is responsibility there is growth. People who are never thrust into responsible positions never develop their real strength. Because they have never been obliged to plan for themselves, they have never developed their powers of originality, inventiveness, initiative, independence, self-reliance, grit, and stamina. The power to create, to make combinations, to meet emergencies, the power which comes from continual marshaling of one's forces to meet difficult situations, to adjust means to ends, that stamina or power which makes one equal to the great crises in the life of a nation or a business, is only developed by years of practical training with great responsibility.

SUM AND SUBSTANCE
- The essence of a team is common commitment. Unless this commitment exists, the members of the group perform as individuals; with it, they become a powerful unit of collective performance.

- Don't boss—lead. You have to stop thinking like a "boss." Bosses make decisions and give orders. Team leaders coordinate groups of thinking adults who together face and work out the problems that face them.

- Successful leaders provide a climate in which their associates are encouraged to make their own analyses of problems, suggest solutions, and participate in decisions. Participation is the key to success.

- To change takes you out of your comfort zone. But progress can't be made unless you become uncomfortable. You have to delve deep into your subconscious mind and cleanse it of old habits and build into it the new ways of doing things.

- The basis for any relationship, on or off the job, is trust. When team members do not trust their leader or one or more of their teammates, the team will never get off the ground.

Chapter Thirteen

Expressing Sincere Appreciation

Everyone wants to be loved and appreciated. Everyone needs to feel important in the world. Realize other people are conscious of their true worth. Like you, they feel the dignity of being an expression of the one life-principle animating all people. As you do this consciously and knowingly, you build up these people and they return your love and goodwill.

In the book of Proverbs, Solomon says: "Be quick to give praise when it is due." And this includes appreciation, courtesy, and civility. We see examples daily of a lack of these manners in many individuals and families. Confucius was correct in saying, "The practices of morality begins with the individual in one's home." It is not unusual to hear "No matter what I do, it is never enough. He (or she) never appreciates it or even says 'Thanks.'"

The obvious question becomes: How often do *you* say, "Thanks, I appreciate you. I think you are a valuable member of our team"? If you want to hear these energizing words, it is wise to say them to others—daily until comfortable—and really mean them. The Golden Rule applied is appreciation in action.

Too often we take our employees and coworkers for granted. We assume that they know we appreciate them and are shocked when they quit to take another job.

When Tony E. left his job with the Building Maintenance Company, he was asked at his exit interview what he liked most and least about the company. Tony responded that, although the salary and benefits were good, he never felt that he was part of the organization. "I always felt that I was looked at as nothing more than a cog in the machine," he said. "During the nine months I worked in the department, I made several suggestions, offered to take on extra projects, and tried to apply creative approaches to some of the work assigned to me. My boss didn't recognize all that I could have contributed."

Had the company recognized Tony's capabilities and shown its appreciation by discussing his suggestions and showing how much the company valued his work, the company would have retained a very valuable employee.

Show Appreciation

William James, the great American psychologist, stated that the deepest urge in human nature is the craving to be appreciated. In our daily lives, both in our personal dealings and on the job, we often forget to express our appreciation to those who make our successes possible.

We tend to look for things to criticize rather than things to compliment. Showing appreciation not only makes the interrelationships on the job much more pleasant, but it builds a spirit of cooperation and collaboration in your team. It makes all of the team more amenable when it is necessary to persuade them to your way of thinking.

Make it a major point to have, at a minimum, a friendly relationship with all of your colleagues and, optimally, a warm and close rapport. One way to accomplish this is to show appreciation to these people for their efforts in anything they do that helps you.

Many business executives feel that an increase in salary or a bonus is a sufficient indication of appreciation for a job well done. Of course, workers do expect tangible rewards for work well done, but money alone is not enough.

A businessman in Maryland told how he did more. One of his employees had consistently produced more than others. He had given above and beyond the call of duty to his job. His bonus was more than the others received, but money did not express the executive's feelings so he wrote him a personal letter of appreciation, which he enclosed with the bonus check. In the letter he thanked him and told him how much he meant to the company. Later the employee thanked him for writing it. He said it made him cry and he would cherish that letter and keep it forever.

During the pre-Thanksgiving rush at Stew Leonard's food market in Norwalk, Connecticut, several office personnel noticed the long, creeping lines at checkout counters and—with no prompting from management—left their regular work duties to help cashiers bag the groceries, which helped speed up the lines.

Stew, the owner of the market, resolved to do something special for the employees who helped out. After the holiday rush was over, he bought each of them a beautifully knitted shirt with the embroidered inscription "Stew Leonard ABCD Award." The inscription stood for "*A*bove and *B*eyond the *C*all of *D*uty." By giving special recognition to associates who did more than their jobs required, he not only gave credit where credit was due but also let everyone—the associates and their coworkers and supervisors, in addition to customers—know that he appreciated the extra effort.

Why Do People Fail to Express Appreciation?

It is often assumed that appreciation is tacitly given when one says "Thank you." Sometimes it is not considered necessary because the other person is "just doing his or her job." Occasionally appreciation is not forthcoming because the person who should express it considers it a sign of weakness or believes it will reflect on his or her own inadequacies. That person may subconsciously think: "If I tell them they did well, they (and others) may feel I am inferior to them." There is no basis for such a conclusion. All great people have repeatedly expressed their gratitude to those who have been helpful to them. In fact, it improves the image of strength they have earned and engenders a higher degree of loyalty among their followers.

One need not be effusive in expressing appreciation. A sincere acknowledgment of how you feel about the work done or the service rendered, or the pride you have in a specific accomplishment, is enough. Nobody ever tires of receiving honest appreciation. Assuming that your appreciation is implied without being expressed is shortchanging the other person. Tell that person that you appreciate what has been done and why you feel that way. In situations that are the result of a specific act, express your appreciation as soon as possible after the completion of this act. Like putting icing on a cake, your expression of appreciation will sweeten the joy of the accomplishment itself.

Appreciation Must Be Sincere

One has to really feel and believe what one is saying for it to come through to the other party as sincere. Insincerity cannot be disguised by fancy words. Your voice, your eyes, and your body language all reflect your true feelings. There is no reason to fake expressions of appreciation. Most of us have so much we do appreciate and so many people who deserve our sincere gratitude.

We should recognize that extra effort put out by our employees or our teammates, that special empathy that we receive from our friends or relatives, or that additional encouragement given to us by our colleagues. The realization that we owe so much to these people should tap the well of true and sincere gratitude that is deep in our hearts. Let it flow. Do not stifle it as it reaches your mouth. Let it spill forth into the ears of those who deserve it, and their lives and yours as well will be a little better that day.

Providing Positive Reinforcement

An autocratic boss continually criticizes, condemns, complains, and never forgets negative performance. But he or she always takes good performance for granted. Managers today have found that reinforcing the good things their associates do rather than harping on their mistakes and inefficiencies has resulted in higher morale and greater productivity.

When people hear continual criticism, they begin to feel stupid, inferior, and resentful. Although someone may have done something that wasn't satisfactory, your objective should be to correct the behavior, not to make the person feel bad.

The famous psychologist B. F. Skinner noted that criticism often reinforces poor behavior (when the only time offenders get attention is when they are being criticized). He recommended that we minimize our reaction to poor behavior and maximize our appreciation of good behavior. When people are constantly criticized, they formulate a pattern of failure that penetrates into their subconscious mind. They look upon themselves as inadequate and this exacerbates their failure rate. To avoid this, replace criticism with guidance.

Rather than bawl out an associate for doing something wrong, quietly tell the person, "You're making some progress in the work, but we still have a long way to go. Let me show you some ways to do it more rapidly." When the work does improve, make a big fuss over it. In this way positive rather than negative thoughts are fed to the subconscious mind.

Some supervisors fear that giving praise indicates softness on their part: "We don't want to coddle our subordinates." Praise is *not* softness—it's a positive approach that reinforces good performance. When you stop thinking of your staff members as subordinates and instead think of them as partners, with you all working to reach the same goals, appropriate praise will become a natural part of your behavior.

Don't Praise Indiscriminately

Human beings thrive on praise. Although all of us require praise to help make us feel good about ourselves, you can't praise people indiscriminately: Praise should be reserved for accomplishments that are worthy of special acknowledgment. So how do you deal with people who never do anything particularly praiseworthy?

Maria C. faced this situation in her group of word processors. Several marginal operators had the attitude that as long as they met their quotas, they were doing okay. Praising them for meeting quotas only reinforced their belief that nothing more was expected of them. Criticism of their failure to do more than the quota required was greeted with the response "I'm doing my job."

Maria decided to try a different kind of positive reinforcement. She gave one of the operators a special assignment for which no production quota had been set. When the job was completed, Maria praised the employee's fine work. She followed this practice with all new assignments and eventually had the opportunity to sincerely praise each of the word processors.

Sometimes we tend to look for things to criticize rather than things to compliment. Because you expect your staff to perform well, you may concentrate on strengthening areas of weakness. Douglas P., a regional supervisor for a California supermarket chain, made regular visits to the eight stores under his jurisdiction. He reported that when he went into a store he looked for *problems*. He criticized store managers for the way products were displayed, for slow-moving checkout lines, and anything else he noticed. "That's my job," he said, "to make sure that everything is being done correctly."

As you can guess, everyone working in the stores dreaded his visits. Douglas's boss acknowledged to him the importance of improving what was wrong but also pointed out that because the stores exceeded sales volume forecasts and kept costs down, the managers needed to hear compliments on their success. His boss suggested that Douglas seek out good things and express his approbation. Douglas was encouraged to make suggestions for improvements, but not to make them the focus of his visits.

Although it wasn't easy, Douglas followed his boss's advice. Within a few months, store managers looked forward to his visits. They began to share new ideas and seek his counsel about store issues. Clerks and other store staffers soon overcame their fear of the "big boss" and welcomed his comments and suggestions.

Five Tips for Effective Praise

As important as praise is in motivating people, it doesn't always work. Some supervisors praise every minor activity, diminishing the value of praise for real accomplishments. Others deliver praise in such a way that it seems phony. To make your praise more meaningful, follow these suggestions:

1. *Don't overdo it.* Praise is sweet. Candy is sweet, too, but the more you eat, the less sweet each piece becomes—and you may get a stomachache. Too much praise reduces the benefit that's derived from each bit of praise; if it's overdone, it loses its value altogether.

2. *Be sincere.* You can't fake sincerity. You must truly believe that what you're praising your associate for is actually commendable. If you don't believe it yourself, neither will your associate.

3. *Be specific about the reason for your praise.* Rather than say, "Great job!" it's much better to say, "The report you submit-

ted on the XYZ matter enabled me to understand more
clearly the complexities of the issue."

4. *Ask for your associate's advice.* Nothing is more flattering
than to be asked for advice about how to handle a situation.
This approach can backfire, though, if you don't *take* the
advice. If you have to reject advice, ask people questions
about their inadequate answers until *they* see the error of
their ways and come up with good advice.

5. *Publicize praise.* Just as a reprimand should always be given
in private, praising should be done (whenever possible) in
public. Sometimes the matter for which praise is given is a
private issue, but often it is appropriate to let your entire
group in on the praise. If other staff members are aware of
the praise you give a colleague, it spurs them to work for
similar recognition.

Make a Fuss Over Achievers

In some cases, praise for significant accomplishments should be
made public, such as at meetings or company events. When praiseworthy accomplishments are publicized and the achievers are lauded
in front of their peers, it encourages others to emulate them.

In Chapter 11, you read about Mary Kay. One way her company has motivated its people is giving recognition to associates
who have accomplished outstanding performance. In addition to
receiving awards and plaques, award winners are feted at company
conventions and publicized in the company magazine. Attending a
Mary Kay convention is similar to attending a victory celebration:
Winners are called to the stage and presented with their awards to
the cheers and applause of an audience. Award winners report that
recognition from senior executives and acclaim from peers is as
rewarding as the award itself.

Give Them Something They Can Keep

Awards vary in most companies from inexpensive plaques or tokens to cash payments, luxury merchandise, or exotic travel.

Mary Kay's highest and most coveted award is her famous pink Cadillacs, given to the highest achievers at the company's award celebrations. To receive this award, salespeople must meet a series of challenges and criteria. It's not easy to win, but every year more Mary Kay associates "make the grade."

Mary Kay doesn't give the cars away. The company leases a car to each winner for one year. In order to keep a car or upgrade to the next year's model, the sales rep must continue to meet the standards. What an incentive to keep up the good work! As a result, relatively few winners have to give up their cars.

It's not necessary to give elaborate gifts like Mary Kay's Cadillacs. No matter what type of award you give employees—large or small—it's worth spending a few more dollars to include a certificate or plaque. Employees love to hang these mementos in their cubicles or offices, over their workbenches, or in their homes. The cash gets spent, the merchandise wears out, the trip becomes a long-past memory, but a certificate or plaque or even just a thank-you note is a permanent reminder of the recognition.

Success Files—The Scorecard

Hillary M., the sales manager of a large real estate office in Florida, makes a practice of sending letters of appreciation to sales staffers who do something special—selling a property that has been difficult to move, obtaining sales rights to a profitable building, or taking creative steps to make a sale.

With the first of these letters that Hillary sends to a salesperson, she encloses a file folder labeled "Success File," with this suggestion: "File the enclosed letter in this folder. Add to it any other commendatory letters you receive from me, from other managers, from clients, or from anyone else. Also record in this file all of your special achievements such as winning sales awards, beating a sales quota, opening a tough new account, etc. As time goes on, you may experience failures or disappointments. There may be times when you don't feel good about yourself. When this happens, reread these letters. They're the proof that you're a success, that you have capability, that you are a special person. You did it before; you can do it again!"

The recipients of Hillary's letters repeatedly tell her how rereading the letters helps them overcome sales slumps, periods of depression, and general disenchantment when things aren't going well. It "reprograms" their psyche by reinforcing their self-esteem, and enables them to face problems with new strength and confidence.

Encourage Peer Recognition

Another successful motivational approach is peer recognition. Companies encourage associates to praise or give formal recognition to colleagues who have made their job easier or more satisfying. One way to do this is to have associates consider other employees with whom they interact as *internal customers* or *internal suppliers*.

Supervisors, managers, and team leaders aren't the only people who see the special efforts their associates make. All team members and coworkers are exposed daily to one another's efforts. Enabling them to recognize the work of peers not only brings to the forefront any accomplishments that may not have been recognized by managers, but also makes both the nominator and the nominee feel that they are part of an integrated, interrelated, and caring organization.

One company that has achieved great results in doing this is Minicircuit Labs, which has plants in Brooklyn, New York, and Hialeah, Florida. This firm provides all its members with "You

Made My Day" forms, on which any employee can write a message of thanks to any coworker, subordinate, or staff member who has earned that employee's special appreciation that day.

At the A&G Merchandising Company in Wilmington, Delaware, team leaders are given packets of thank-you cards on which the words "Thank You" are printed in beautiful script on the front flap and the inside of the card is left blank. Whenever someone does something worthy of special recognition, that person's team leader writes a note on one of the cards detailing the special accomplishment and congratulating the employee for achieving it. The recipients cherish the cards and show them to friends and family.

SUM AND SUBSTANCE

- Nobody ever tires of receiving honest appreciation. Assuming that your appreciation is implied without being expressed is shortchanging the other person. Tell that person that you appreciate what has been done and why you feel that way.

- When people hear continual criticism, they begin to feel stupid, inferior, and resentful. Although someone may have done something that wasn't satisfactory, your objective should be to correct the behavior, not to make the person feel bad.

- When people are constantly criticized, they formulate a pattern of failure that penetrates into their subconscious mind. They look upon themselves as inadequate, and this exacerbates their failure rate. To avoid this, replace criticism with guidance. Rather than bawl out an associate for doing something wrong, quietly tell the person, "You're making some progress in the work. Let me show you some ways to do it more rapidly." When the work does improve, make a big fuss over it. In this way positive rather than negative thoughts are fed to the subconscious mind.

- Praise is *not* softness—it's a positive approach that reinforces good performance. When you stop thinking of your staff members as subordinates and instead think of them as partners all working to reach the same goals, appropriate praise will become a natural part of your behavior.

- Praise should be reserved for accomplishments that are worthy of special acknowledgment.

- By focusing on positive things—by giving attention and appreciation to the good things people do—you reinforce their desire to do the right thing.

- When praiseworthy accomplishments are publicized and the achievers are lauded in front of their peers, it encourages others to emulate them.

- Encourage associates to praise or give formal recognition to colleagues who have made their job easier or more satisfying.

Chapter Fourteen

Communicating More Effectively

People who can talk well, who have the art of putting things in an attractive way, who can interest others immediately by their power of speech, have a very great advantage over those who may know more but who cannot express themselves with ease or eloquence.

In order to get things done, we have to communicate with the people we work with. Without words, whether orally or in writing, no job could be accomplished.

However, it's not just what we say, but how we say it (or perhaps write it) that will determine whether our words lead to the actions we desire. We have to make sure that the people we communicate with not only understand what we are saying—whether it be an order, a suggestion, or an idea—but also accept it.

These days, *communication*—what you say and how you say it—can determine whether you succeed or fail. Take Ronald Reagan, for example. Many Americans believe that his chief attribute was his ability to communicate with voters so effectively (and telegenically).

This skill, shared by the most successful professionals, business executives, and government leaders, is a skill you, too, can acquire. All you need is will and determination. Once you've improved your ability to communicate, you can more effectively present your ideas to your boss, your associates, your customers, your team, even your friends and family.

Word power is greater than thermonuclear weapons or atomic bombs, for the simple reason that words decree whether these weapons are to be used or remain latent. Word power may be used to order atomic power to drive a ship across an ocean or to devastate a city or a nation. At a seminar on improving communication skills, the participants were told that words would produce fabulous results for them. It was suggested that they take certain words that appealed to them and verbally repeat them over and over for about ten or more minutes twice a day. Or if they preferred, write down what they were wishing to accomplish and mentally go over these statements from time to time, thereby gradually conveying the ideas to their subconscious minds.

One of the participants, an insurance salesman, claimed boldly: "I am now attracting only those men and women who are interested and who have the money to invest for their children's education and for their own welfare." His persistent use of these affirmative words has attracted to him more interested people than ever before. Leads now come to him seemingly from nowhere, and he has made tremendous strides on the scale of life and in all its varied phases.

Good Communication Requires Preparation

Whether you're addressing a group or having a one-on-one conversation, you should think out your message and how you plan to present it in advance. Sometimes you'll have to think on your feet with little or no time to prepare, but more often than not when you're required to discuss something, you *can* prepare—even on short notice.

Know Your Subject

On the job, you'll usually communicate with others about subjects you're thoroughly familiar with: the work you're doing, matters in your own area of expertise, or company-related problems. Still, you should review the facts to be sure that you have a handle on all the available information and are prepared to answer any questions.

From time to time, you may be asked to report on matters with which you are unfamiliar. Your company may want to purchase a new type of computer software, for example, and ask you to check it out. Here's how you should start tackling such assignments:

- Learn as much as possible about the subject.

- Know considerably more than you think you ought to know for the presentation.

- Prepare notes about the pros and cons of the proposed purchase, solution, and so on.

- Whether you will make this report to one person (your boss, for example) or to a group of managers or technical specialists, be prepared to answer questions about any subject that might come up.

Know Your Audience

Half of good communication is understanding your audience. Even the most skilled orators will fail to communicate effectively if their audience can't understand them. Choose words that your listeners will easily comprehend. If the people you address come from a technical background, you can use technical terminology that your listeners will clearly and readily understand. But if you talk about technical subject matter to an audience unfamiliar with it, drop the technical language. If your listeners can't understand your vocabulary, your message will be lost.

Dennis K., an engineer, was asked to explain a concept he had developed to a group of financiers from whom he hoped to obtain the financing for his company's project. He sought advice from his boss. "I have no trouble communicating my ideas to other engineers," he said. "We speak the same language, but these bankers come from another world. I am terribly afraid they won't understand me at all."

His boss told him that it was his responsibility, not the bankers', to ensure that his message got across. He must translate the technical matter into layperson's terms. If it was essential to use technical language, he should take the time to explain a term the first time he used it and at least once again if he felt that it needed reinforcement.

Dennis followed that advice and his boss and his colleagues complimented him on his presentation, which led to the bankers' financing of the project.

On the other hand, do not talk down to an audience. Bernard R., a human relations attorney, was retained by a major company to train their factory supervisors on the latest equal employment laws and regulations. Bernard assumed that the supervisors were totally unfamiliar with the laws and spent the entire morning on the basics. He noticed that the participants looked bored and restless. It wasn't until the lunch break that he learned that they had recently attended a seminar on the laws and had expected him to explain the more complex aspects of interpreting and implementing them. Sure, the manager who retained him should have told him, but good communicators make it their business to learn as much about the background of their listeners and the level of their knowledge of the subject, so they can communicate effectively.

Be Aware of Body Language

In communicating your thoughts, it is not only what you say but what your body says that conveys your message. People communicate not only through words but also through their facial expressions and body movements. If there were only a dictionary of body language, we could easily interpret what those signs signify. But because body language isn't standardized like verbal language, no such dictionary could be written.

Our cultural or ethnic background, the way our parents expressed themselves nonverbally, and other individual experiences influence the way we use our bodies. Body language differs from one person to another. Some gestures—a nod or a smile—may seem universal, but not everyone uses body language in the same way. When you're dealing with a specific person, you can't be sure that he or she is giving the signals you have come to expect.

For example, as you talk, your listener is nodding. Good—you assume that he or she is agreeing with you. Not necessarily so. There are some people who nod just to acknowledge that they're listening. When someone folds his or her arms as you speak, you might think the action is a subconscious show of disagreement, but it could simply be that that person is cold! There is danger in misreading nonverbal cues.

Take the time to learn each person's body language. Study the body language of people with whom you work. You may notice that when John smiles in a certain way, it has one meaning; a different smile, a different meaning. Or maybe when Jane doesn't agree, she wrinkles her forehead. Make a conscious effort to study and remember people's individual body language.

Are you aware of your own body language? One way to see how you project your message is to rehearse in front of a mirror. You may see gestures, expressions, or movements that detract from your message or even contradict your verbal statements. A more effective way is to have somebody videotape an actual presentation that you make. By carefully studying it, you will be able to identify and correct wrong impressions and reinforce gestures that strengthen your points.

Are You Really Listening?

Suppose one of your colleagues brings a problem to you and asks for help. You begin listening attentively, but before you know it, your mind is wandering. Instead of listening to the problem, you're thinking about the pile of work on your desk, the meeting you have scheduled with the company vice president, the scuffle your son got into at school. You hear your colleague's words, but you're not really listening.

Does this happen to you? Of course, it does. It happens to all of us. Why? Our minds can process ideas ten times faster than we can talk. While someone is talking, your mind may race ahead. You complete the speaker's sentence in your mind—often incorrectly— long before he or she does. You "hear" what your mind dictates, not what's actually said. This is human nature. But that's no excuse for being a bad listener.

Now suppose your mind was wandering and you didn't hear what the other person said. It's embarrassing to admit you weren't listening, so you fake it. You pick up on the last few words you heard and comment on them. If you make sense, you're lucky. But you may have missed the real gist of the discussion.

When you haven't been listening, you don't have to admit, "I'm sorry, I was daydreaming." One way to get back on track is to ask a question or make a comment about the last item you did hear: "Can we go back a minute to such-and-such?" Another method is to comment this way: "To make sure I can better understand your view on this, please elaborate."

Become an Active Listener

Of course, it is far better to train your mind to avoid daydreaming and push away distractions.

Agnes Gund was president of the Museum of Modern Art, the largest modern-art museum in the United States, when they planned a major redesign of the building, to the tune of $800 million. She had to work with every department to assure that they all agreed, even if they didn't start out with the same thoughts. Gund had to develop skills to persuade people to understand her point of view and to accept what she thought would work best. She recognized that she had a tendency not to fully listen to others, and realized that although she was an expert on art, she lacked expertise in construction. Ms. Gund understood the power of the subconscious mind and she meditated on her need to pay full attention and concentrate on what the construction specialists were telling her. The result was successful completion of the project with a minimum of tension.

In addition to programming your subconscious mind to open up to what others are saying, you can take some active steps to improve your listening skills. Instead of just sitting or standing with your ears open, follow these guidelines:

- *Look at the speaker.* Eye contact is one way of showing interest, but don't overdo it. Look at the whole person; don't just stare into his or her eyes.

- *Show interest through your facial expressions.* Smile or show concern when appropriate.

- *Indicate that you are following the conversation by nods or gestures.*

- *Ask questions about what's being said.* You can paraphrase— "So the way I understand it is . . ."—or ask specific questions about particular points. This technique not only enables you to clarify points that may be unclear, but also keeps you alert and paying full attention.

- *Don't interrupt.* A pause should not be a signal for you to start talking. Wait.

Be Empathetic

One cause for our conversational decline is a lack of empathy. We are too selfish, too busily engaged in our own welfare and wrapped up in our own little world, too intent upon our own self-promotion to be interested in others. No one can make a good conversationalist who is not empathetic. To be a good listener or a good talker, you must be able to enter into another's life, to live it with the other person for a while, and you must touch the people you are conversing with along the lines of their interest. No matter how much you may know about a subject, if it does not happen to interest those to whom you are talking, your efforts will be largely lost.

Facilitate Communication

Many companies have invested in complex and expensive communication systems to enable them to deal with customers more rapidly and effectively, but to a great extent, technology has dehumanized organizations and made dealing with these organizations not just unpleasant but often frustrating. It defeats the main purpose of communication—speed, ease, and pleasantness in dealing with customers and the public.

Clients and customers are universally fed up with automated telephone routing systems that put callers on hold and sometimes cut them off. Companies in highly competitive situations spend millions on advertising, but miss the boat when a potential customer is calling. A company's unwillingness to open the lines of communication between themselves and their customers sends the undesirable message that "customers don't count."

Unfortunately, few companies have even tried to solve this problem, because they believe the positives—lower cost and ability to deal with routine matters more systematically—outweigh the negatives. One business executive who felt it important that his staff maintain personal contact with customers is Bob Kierlin,

founder and chairman of Fastenal, a leading U.S. distributor of industrial products. He answers his own phone and books appoint-
ments immediately during the conversation. He has no gatekeepers,
no rude assistants or PR people, and he built a $2 billion company
with two thousand stores. When asked his secret, he talks about
what some consider "little things," such as communication, making yourself available. It's not only Kierlin who communicates,
however. The business press reports that members of his staff respond exactly the same way. They actually return phone calls.

Rejecting Suggestions Without Causing Resentment

Another barrier to good communication is the fear many people
have that if they make a suggestion the boss disagrees with, it will
demean them in his or her eyes. Rather than face such rejection,
they keep their ideas to themselves. On the other side of this coin is
the fact that some supervisors are reluctant to reject even poor
ideas from subordinates for fear that rejection of one idea may
discourage them from future contributions.

You cannot think this way. You must encourage those with
whom you work or deal with to express their ideas and offer suggestions. You must learn to reject poor suggestions diplomatically
so as not to cause resentment. Here are some ideas on how to reject poor suggestions in a positive manner:

- *Do it privately.* Never reject a person's suggestion in front of
others. It causes them to lose face and be embarrassed in front
of their peers. Thank them for the suggestion and tell them
you will get back to them. Even if it appears unworkable,
study it. You may be wrong. And do get back with your answer as soon as possible.

- *Give them the reason—and listen to their response.* Typically
when you get suggestions that appear to be obviously flawed,

you might say, if true, "We tried that before and it didn't work." A better approach is to phrase it like this: "We tried something like that two years ago and we had some problems with it."

Note the difference in the choice of words. The first comment, "It didn't work," was final. It left no door open for the other person to respond. The second approach, "We had some problems with it," keeps the door open. The most likely response that can be made to that comment is "What were the problems?" Once the other person learns what caused the previous failure, he or she may respond, "I didn't think about that. I guess I should give this some more thought." Instead of repressing future ideas, you have encouraged the person to keep thinking, or perhaps he or she does have a valid idea: "I thought about those problems and I have solutions." One of the advantages of collaboration is that you accept that you don't have all the answers yourself and that others may see things in a situation that have escaped you.

• *The Socratic approach.* Rather than overtly reject an idea, question the person who suggested it. This is how Socrates stimulated his pupils to think things out. He never told one of his students that he was wrong. If one of his students came up with a wrong answer, Socrates asked another question. By carefully wording the questions, this great teacher encouraged his pupils to think out the problem and through this thought process reach the right solution.

This is still called the "Socratic approach." By careful questioning you can stimulate the person who made the suggestion to rethink and reevaluate his or her idea and come up with a more viable suggestion. In this way, you never have to reject an idea. There is no resentment, and continued encouragement of employee ideation will result from this method. As noted earlier in this chapter, another benefit of asking questions is that it enables you to become a better listener.

Disagreeing Without Being Disagreeable

Some people are very sensitive. They cannot accept criticism easily and become defensive when one of their ideas is turned down. Let's say that one of your associates has spent several days developing a new program and has brought it to you, for what he or she expects will be not just approval, but congratulations. You find that although it has many good points, the new program has several areas that need significant improvement.

How can you convey this without causing this sensitive person to blow up, become resentful, and perhaps sulk for days?

Instead of pointing out the areas with which you disagree, first compliment your associate on all of the good points in the program. Then instead of pointing out your objections, ask specific questions on each area of disagreement. There are three possible responses that can be made to your questions.

One response: "I hadn't thought about that. I had better review this and come up with a better approach." This response shows that you have encouraged your associate to do what has to be done to make the program more workable.

Another possible response: "I hadn't thought about that. What should I do?" This type of response indicates that your associate agrees that the concept was not right, but instead of trying to solve it, he or she throws the problem back to you to solve. It is tempting to tell your associate what to do—and if it is a crisis situation, you may have to do this to get the job done on time. However, it is best to encourage people to solve their own problems. Your response should be: "Why don't you give this some more thought and we'll talk about it later in the week."

A third response: Your associate answers your question and you realize that he or she was right and your objection was not valid. In this case, thank your associate for clarifying the matter and go on to your next question.

By questioning rather than criticizing, we can get the best from people without resentment. The employee rejects his or her own bad ideas and is encouraged to come up with better ones. This will result in the honing of your partners' creative skills and in obtaining more innovative ideas that will increase the effectiveness of your department.

Communication Is a Two-Way Street

We send out our messages to others, but we are also receiving messages from them. We must learn how to encourage others to share their ideas, and more important, we must learn to truly listen to what is told to us. To be effective, feedback must flow from one party to the other on a continuous basis. The sender of the message must always ensure that what is sent is understood and accepted by the receiver. To accomplish this, the sender must ask questions, observe what is observable, and if there are misunderstandings, correct them and ensure that the corrections are understood. He or she must seek the acceptance of the communication by the receiver so that there will be a sincere willingness to accomplish what is desired.

If you follow these fundamentals of good communication, not only will your messages get across more readily, but work will be accomplished in a more timely fashion.

SUM AND SUBSTANCE
- Good communicators have trained their subconscious minds to give them the power and capability of projecting their ideas, their wishes, their deepest concerns to others, and it has resulted in the success of their endeavors.

- Half of good communication is understanding your audience. Choose words that your listeners will easily comprehend. If your listeners can't understand your vocabulary, your message will be lost.

- Body language differs from one person to another. When you're dealing with an individual, you can't be sure that he or she is giving the signals you have come to expect. Make a conscious effort to study and remember people's individual body language.

- Be an active listener. Instead of just sitting or standing with your ears open, follow these guidelines:
  - Look at the speaker.
  - Show interest by your facial expressions. Indicate that you are following the conversation by nods or gestures.
  - Ask questions about what's being said.
  - Don't interrupt.
  - Be empathetic. You must be able to enter into another's life, to live it with the other person for a while, to be a good listener or a good talker.

- Good communicators bring listeners close to them. They open their hearts wide and exhibit a broad, free nature and an open mind.

- In rejecting suggestions from others, do not criticize or condemn them, use the Socratic approach. Ask good questions and they will realize their own mistakes.

- For communication to be effective there must be feedback flowing from one party to the other on a continuous basis. The sender of the message must always ensure that what is sent is understood and accepted by the receiver.

Chapter Fifteen

Dealing with Difficult People

Your subconscious mind is a recording machine that reproduces your habitual thinking. Think good of others and you are actually thinking good about yourself.

There is no problem in human relations that you cannot solve harmoniously and for the benefit of all concerned. When you say that your associate in the office is very difficult to handle, that he or she is cantankerous, mean, obstreperous, and difficult, do you realize that in all probability this is reflecting your own inner mental states? Remember also that like attracts like. Is it not possible that your associate's crotchety, petulant, critical attitude is the reflection of your inner frustrations and suppressed rage? What this person says or does cannot really hurt you unless you permit him or her to mentally disturb you. The only way that person can annoy you is through your own thoughts.

This is because you are the only thinker in your universe. You and you alone are responsible for the way you think about other people. They are not responsible, you are. For example, if you get angry, you have to go through four states in your own mind. You begin to think about what the other person said. You decide to get angry and generate a mood of rage. Then you decide to act. Perhaps you talk back and react in kind. It takes two to make an argument. Notice that the thought, emotion, reaction, and action all take place in your own mind. You and you alone are responsible.

Whatever you believe is true in your conscious mind your subconscious will accept without question. Be very careful that you accept only that which is true, noble, and Godlike.

"Everybody Annoys Me"

Henry F. couldn't understand why everybody around him annoyed him. He talked about this to a counselor. The counselor pointed out that Henry was constantly rubbing others the wrong way. He did not like himself and was full of self-condemnation. He spoke in a very tense, irritable tone. His acerbity of speech grated on everyone's nerves. He thought meanly of himself and was highly critical of others.

The counselor explained to him that while his unhappy experiences seemed to be with other people, his relationship with them was determined by his thoughts and feelings about himself and them. If he despised himself, he could not have goodwill and respect for others. It's impossible, because it is a law of mind that people always project their thoughts and feelings onto their associates and all those around them.

Henry began to realize that as long as he projected feelings of prejudice, ill will, and contempt for others, that is exactly what he would get back, because his world was but an echo of his moods and attitudes.

The counselor suggested that he write the following thoughts in his subconscious mind. Remember, your conscious mind is the pen, and with it you can write anything you want in your subconscious mind. This is what Henry wrote:

Practice the Golden Rule from now on, which means that I think, speak, and act toward others as I wish others to think, speak, and act toward me. I sincerely wish peace, prosperity, and success to all. I am always poised, serene, and calm. Others appreciate and respect me as I appreciate myself. Life is honoring me greatly, for it has provided for me abundantly. The petty things of life no longer irritate me or annoy me. When fear, worry, doubt, or criticism by others come to me and knock at my door, faith, goodness, truth, and beauty open the door of my mind. There is no one there. The suggestions and statements of others have no power. I know now how to cure hurt feelings. The only power is in my own thought.

Henry affirmed these truths morning, noon, and night, and he committed the whole prayer to memory. He poured into these words life, love, and meaning. By osmosis these ideas penetrated the layers of his subconscious mind, and he became a changed man. He reported, "I am learning how to specialize myself out of the law of averages. I am getting along fine. I have received a promotion on my job. I now know the truth of the passage: 'If I be lifted up in my mind, I will draw all manifestation unto me.'"

He learned that the trouble was within himself. He decided to change his thoughts, feelings, and reactions. Anyone can do the same. It takes decision, perseverance, and the keen desire to transform oneself.

Return Good for Evil

It should not come as a surprise that some people in the world are difficult. Many people in our everyday lives are often argumentative, uncooperative, cantankerous, cynical, and sour on life. Some are sick psychologically. Their minds have become deformed and distorted, perhaps because of experiences they have had in the past. Others may be stressed by their work or by personal problems.

What do you do when you have to deal with someone like this? The temptation is to turn their negative energy back on them in the form of dislike. But to do that, you first have to take their negativity into yourself, with all the bad effects that will have on your own being. Strive instead to "return good for evil." This creates an armor that keeps their difficult and unpleasant attitudes from affecting you, and your transmission of compassion and understanding will set in motion the process of changing them.

Mrs. Wrong Way was jealous and hateful toward the supervisor in her office. She was suffering from hurt feelings. She had developed ulcers and high blood pressure. Once she became aware of the spiritual principle of forgiveness and goodwill, she realized that she had accumulated many resentful and grudging attitudes and that these negative and obnoxious thoughts were festering in her subconscious mind. She tried to talk with Ms. Supervisor in an effort to straighten matters out, but the woman brushed her off. In a continuing effort to correct the situation, Mrs. Wrong Way reinforced the principles of harmony and goodwill for ten minutes every night and every morning prior to going to work. This is what she did. She affirmed as follows: "I surround Ms. Supervisor with harmony, love, peace, joy, and goodwill."

Now, this is not mumbo jumbo. She knew what she was doing and why she was doing it. These thoughts or ideas sink into the subconscious. There is only one subconscious mind, and the other person picks it up. She said, "There is harmony, peace, and understanding between us. Whenever I think of Ms. Supervisor, I will say, 'God's love saturates your mind.'"

A few weeks passed, and Mrs. Wrong Way went on a business trip to San Francisco. On boarding the plane, she discovered that the only vacant seat was the one next to Ms. Supervisor. Mrs. Wrong Way greeted her cordially and received a cordial response.

They had a harmonious and joyous time together in San Francisco. They are now friends and their working relationship has so improved that both have received promotions.

Infinite Intelligence set the stage for the solution to this difficulty in ways that Mrs. Wrong Way didn't know. Mrs. Wrong Way's changed thinking had changed everything, including a perfect healing of her ulcers and high blood pressure. She was hurting herself. No other person is responsible for how you think or feel; you are, because you are the only thinker in your universe. Only you are responsible for the way you think about others.

Change Your Mind-Set

Lee Y., a waiter in the restaurant of a luxury hotel in Hawaii, reported how he dealt with a particularly ornery patron. Every year an eccentric millionaire from the mainland visited the hotel. This visitor proved to be a miserly type who hated to give a waiter or bellboy a tip. He was churlish, ill-mannered, rude, and just plain unpleasant. Nothing satisfied him. He was constantly complaining about the food and the service. He snarled at the waiters whenever he was served.

Lee reported, "I realized he was a sick man. A kahuna [native Hawaiian priest] told me that when people are like that, there is something eating them inside. So I decided to kill him with kindness." Lee consistently treated this man with courtesy, kindness, and respect, silently affirming, "God loves him and cares for him. I see God in him, and he sees God in me." He practiced this technique for about a month, at the end of which time this eccentric millionaire for the first time said, "Good morning, Lee. How's the weather? You are the best waiter I have ever had." Lee was astounded. "I almost fainted," he said. I expected a growl, and I got a compliment. He gave me $500 as a parting tip."

A word is a thought expressed. Lee's words and thoughts were addressed to the subconscious mind of the cranky, cantankerous guest. They gradually melted the ice in his heart. He responded in love and kindness.

"My Deskmate Is a Slob"

Sandy L., a part-time art director, shared a desk with another part-timer who had a habit of leaving the desk a mess when he left. She asked the human resources director how to get her deskmate to be neater. The director suggested: "Ask him to neaten up, sure. But to keep things businesslike and cooperative, talk with him *in person*, rather than leaving a note, even if it means going to the office on your day off. Try saying, 'It would be really helpful if you could clear up the desk for me before you leave. Otherwise I'm concerned that I might accidentally lose some of your paperwork.'"

Sandy reported back that this technique for solving a problem without creating another one had worked so well that the other part-timer established separate inboxes for the two of them, and the desk was now cleared each day. What could have been a cause for resentment was handled in a collegial fashion, which took a bit more time and effort, but was well worth it.

Dealing with Negative Personalities

If you supervise others, you will inevitably run into negative attitudes in your group at some point. Every team leader or supervisor does. They can make your life miserable or make it an ever-changing challenge. You can't ignore negativity—you have to deal with it.

Negative personalities also aren't reserved for supervisors. Almost every organization has a Negative Nell or Ned at all levels of the corporate ladder. They could be coworkers, important customers, government regulators, or anyone else with whom you have to deal. Whenever you're for something, they're against it. They always have a reason that what you want to accomplish just can't be done. They can tear down your team with pessimism.

A person's negativity may stem from some real or perceived past mistreatment by your company. If that's the case, look into the matter. If the person has justifiable reasons for being negative, try to persuade him or her that the past is past and to look to the future. If misconceptions are involved, try to clear them up.

In dealing with negative people, acknowledge their arguments and persuade them to work with you to overcome their perceived problems so that the project can move along. Make the person part of the solution rather than an additional problem.

Opal is one of those people who exude negativity. It's not what she says—it's how she acts. She takes any suggestion as a personal affront and takes on any new assignment with such reluctance and annoyance that she turns everyone off.

People such as Opal often don't realize how they come across to others. They probably act this way in their personal lives as well as on the job. They're the type of people who don't get along with their families, have few friends, and are forever the dissenters. If you have people like Opal on your team, have a heart-to-heart talk with them to let them know how their attitude affects your team's morale. Amazingly, many negative-thinking people have no idea that their behavior is disruptive to others. They must learn how to push negativity out of their subconscious mind by building positive thoughts into their conscious mind.

Reread Chapter 3 and help Opal and others like her to apply the suggestions made on how to change a negative attitude into a positive, affirmative, self-confident approach to one's career and indeed to one's entire life.

Employee Assistance Programs

An employee assistance program, or EAP, is a company-sponsored counseling service. Many companies have instituted these programs to help employees deal with personal problems that interfere with productivity. The counselors aren't company employees, but instead are outside experts retained on an as-needed basis. Use of the EAP can be initiated in two ways.

Sometimes an employee takes the initiative in contacting the company's EAP. The company informs its employees about the program through email, bulletins, and announcements in the company newspaper, meetings, and letters to their homes. Often a hotline telephone number is provided.

For example, Gerty believed that she needed help. Constant squabbling with her teenage daughter had made her tense, angry, and frustrated. It was interfering with her concentration on her job and she had occasionally lost her temper in dealing with co-workers.

She took advantage of the EAP program and phoned the "hotline." A screening counselor listened to Gerty's problem and referred her to a family counselor. Gerty made her own appointment on her own time—not during working hours. EAPs are not an excuse for taking time off the job. Because the entire procedure is confidential, no report was made to the company about Gerty's counseling. In most cases, not even the names of people who undertake counseling are divulged.

Another way the process can be started is by having a supervisor take the initiative to contact the EAP. Suppose the work performance of one of the supervisor's top performers has recently declined. The supervisor often sees this employee sitting idly at his or her desk, thoughts obviously far from the job. The supervisor asks the employee what's going on, but he or she shrugs off the question by saying, "I'm okay—just tired." After several conversations, the employee finally admits to a family problem. At this point the supervisor may suggest that the employee contact the company's EAP.

Even though a supervisor made the referral and the employee has followed through, there are no progress reports. From now on, the matter is handled confidentially. Feedback comes from seeing improvement in the employee's work as the counseling helps with the problem.

Employee assistance programs are expensive to maintain, but organizations that have used them for several years report that they pay off. EAPs salvage skilled and experienced workers who, without help, may leave a company.

Tampering with Temper Tantrums

Terry is a good worker, but from time to time he loses his temper and hollers and screams at his coworkers. He calms down quickly, but his behavior affects the work of the entire team, and it takes awhile to get back to normal performance.

It's not easy to work in an environment in which people holler and scream. It disrupts the work not only of the persons directly involved, but of all people in the work area. They may be unable to work at full capacity for several hours afterward. This situation cannot be tolerated. It is usually the responsibility of the supervisor or team leader to deal with these situations, but sometimes, a trusted coworker may intervene to calm the person down without need for more formal action.

Here are some suggestions for dealing with someone who has temper tantrums:

- After the person calms down, the supervisor or, where appropriate, a senior employee or representative from the human resources department should have a heart-to-heart talk with him or her. Point out that it is understandable that it's not always easy for someone to control his or her temper, but that such tantrums aren't acceptable in the workplace.

- If another outburst occurs, the person should be sent out of the room until he or she can calm down. Let the person know that the next offense will lead to disciplinary action.

- If the person being criticized begins to cry or throw a tantrum, walk out! Wait ten minutes, and then try again. Assure the person that this isn't a personal attack but a means of correcting a situation. Note: Private offices are not good places to conduct these types of meetings. It's not a good idea to leave an upset person alone in an office. There have been situations where the upset employee trashed an office in anger. Use a conference room instead. Of course, workers who become physically disruptive must be removed from the premises and disciplinary action be taken.

- Termination is, of course, the ultimate action. People who have frequent temper tantrums should not be kept on the payroll. Supervisors must follow company policies and, where appropriate, union contracts when taking this step.

Playing "Gotcha"

Have you ever worked with an associate whose greatest joy in life is to catch other people making an error? People who play this game are trying to show their superiority. Because they usually have no original ideas or constructive suggestions, they get their kicks from catching other people's errors, whether it be a coworker or their boss. They try to embarrass the other person and make him or her uncomfortable. If you are the person who is being challenged, don't give this person the satisfaction of playing the game. Make a joke about it ("What a blooper!"), or smile and say, "Thanks for calling it to my attention before it caused real problems." If those "gotchamongers" see that you're not riled by their game, they'll stop and try to get their kicks elsewhere.

Working with Unhappy People

There's likely to be at least one unhappy person in your group. We all experience periods when things go wrong at home or on the job—and it affects the way we do our work and how we interact with other staff members. Supervisors should be alert to this likelihood and take the time to chat with the person. Giving a person the opportunity to talk about a problem often alleviates the tension. Even if the problem isn't solved, it clears the air and enables the associate to function normally.

Some people, however, will always be unhappy about something. They often aren't satisfied with work assignments. Even when you comply with their requests and accommodate their complaints, they're not satisfied. They display their unhappiness by being negative. If someone's request for a change in scheduling a vacation is denied, for example, that person may get angry and let it show both overtly and subtly in his or her attitude.

You can never make everyone happy. Rebuilding the morale of people who believe that they've been treated unfairly takes tact and patience. Managers can avoid some unfair situations by making sure—at the time a decision is made—to explain the reasons behind the decision. In the vacation example, you could explain that your company sets up the vacation schedule months in advance and that two other employees are taking their vacations at the same time. Then make it clear that your group can't spare more than one member on vacation at a time. You may even suggest that the unhappy person try to find another staff member who will trade vacation time.

Dealing with an unhappy coworker is more complex than dealing with a subordinate, because you have no real power to correct the situation that may be the cause of the unhappiness. One way of alleviating the problem is to be an attentive and empathetic listener and to help that person accept the situation. A heart-to-heart talk often is most helpful. This is especially true when the person initiating the conversation is a good friend or an empathetic colleague.

Eva S. was that kind of person. She was looked upon as the foster mother of her work group. She was the one to whom her coworkers brought their problems—both personal and job-related. She was a good listener and although she didn't always solve the problems, she opened a channel for them to vent their concerns and often helped them think the problems through more carefully.

Some people find guidance by meditation or prayer. One prayer that has been a great help to thousands of people is Dr. Reinhold Niebuhr's serenity prayer: "God grant me the serenity to accept the things I cannot change, the courage to change the things I can and the wisdom to know the difference."

Unhappiness, like negativity, results from lack of self-esteem. You can help others—whether they be subordinates or coworkers—by helping them develop higher self-esteem. In Chapter 2 of this book, you will find many ideas on how to do this in a general way.

As a manager, you can help by focusing on successes, not on failures. Most people don't loathe themselves, but they may have temporary self-esteem slumps and need bolstering. If they don't deal with those slumps, more serious consequences can occur. Most people don't need professional care; they can do it themselves.

Loss of self-esteem stems from failure. All of us have failures and successes in our jobs and in our lives.

When you focus on failure, self-esteem deteriorates. Concentrate instead on the successes that have been achieved. Here are some suggestions:

- Keep a success log (see Chapter 13). Have the unhappy worker enter in this log any accomplishments he or she is especially proud of—things for which the worker has been commended. These things prove that the unhappy worker succeeded in the past and serve as assurance that he or she can succeed again.

- Give employees with low self-esteem positive reinforcement for every achievement, and praise for progress made in their work. Equally important, be positive when they come up with a good idea or make meaningful contributions to team discussions and activities. People with low self-esteem need to be continually reminded that you, the supervisor, respect them and have confidence in them.

- Give them assignments you know they can handle, and provide added training, coaching, and support to ensure that they'll succeed. The taste of success is a surefire way to build self-esteem.

- Suggest that they take courses designed to build self-confidence, or assertiveness training programs. Provide them with inspirational tapes or books.

These suggestions will reinforce employees' positive thinking about themselves in their subconscious mind and work wonders in overcoming defeatist attitudes.

SUM AND SUBSTANCE
- As long as you project feelings of prejudice, ill will, and contempt for others, that is exactly what you will get back, because your world is but an echo of your moods and attitudes.

- Chronic complainers may just be seeking attention. To ward off some of their complaints, give them the opportunity to express themselves on a regular basis.

- Be empathetic. If you are a supervisor, let your staff know you are willing to listen to whatever is on their minds. If you are not in a supervisory position, you can still be of help to your colleagues by opening your heart to their concerns.

• When a person has a serious problem, beyond your capability to help, refer that person to someone who can. Company employee assistance programs are one source of such help.

• When dealing with difficult people, the temptation is to turn their negative energy back on them in the form of dislike. But to do that, you first have to take their negativity into yourself, with all the bad effects that will have on your own being.

• In dealing with negative people, acknowledge their arguments and persuade them to work with you to overcome their perceived problems so that the project can move along. Make the person part of the solution rather than an additional problem.

Chapter Sixteen

Managing Your Time

Stop writing blank checks, such as, "There is not time enough to go around," or "There is too much to do," etc. Such statements magnify and multiply your loss.

Suppose somebody came to you and said, "I will give you $86,400 a day every day, but you must spend it all each day." You will get no more and no less every day. You cannot keep it or save it. Wouldn't that be a wonderful gift? God gives each of us a similar gift—86,400 seconds each day of our lives. We must use up those seconds each day. We cannot keep them or save them. We can throw those seconds away on frivolous pursuits or let them fly by doing nothing. Or we can use them to develop our minds, to work or to play, to be with our friends and families, to help other people. Use this gift well. It is a gift from God.

Controlling Your Time

Many of us are unaware of the power we have over controlling our use of time. We are like the poor woman who had lived for all her life in the back country. She moved to a progressive little village where, to her great surprise, she found that her new home was lighted by electricity. She knew nothing about electricity, had never even seen an electric light before, and the little eight-candlepower electric bulbs with which the house was fitted seemed very marvelous to her.

Later, a man came along one day, selling a new kind of electric bulb, and asked the woman to allow him to replace one of her small bulbs with one of his new style sixty-candlepower bulbs just to show her what it would do. She consented, and when the electricity was turned on she stood transfixed. It seemed to her nothing short of magical that such a little bulb could give so wonderful a light, almost like that of sunlight. She never dreamed that the source of the new flood of illumination had been there all the time; that the enormously increased light came from the same current, which had been feeding her little eight-candlepower bulb.

We smile at the ignorance of this poor woman, but the majority of us are far more ignorant of our own power than she was of the power of the electric current. We go through life using a little eight-candlepower bulb, believing we are getting all the power that can come to us, all that we can express or that destiny will give us, believing that we are limited to eight-candlepower bulbs. We never dream that an infinite current, a current in which we are perpetually bathed, would flood our lives with light, with a light inconceivably brilliant and beautiful, if we would only put in a larger bulb, make a larger connection with the infinite supply current. The supply wire we are using is so tiny that only a little of the great current can flow through, only a few candlepower, when there are millions flowing past our very door. An unlimited supply of this infinite current is ours for the taking, ours for the expressing.

Our time is like that current. Many of us are content to use it like the eight-candlepower bulb, when we have within us the potential to use our time much more effectively. Just as changing to a brighter bulb can give us more brilliant light, so can changing our management of time enable us to accomplish much more in our lives.

Set Time-Related Goals

The first step in good time management is establishing goals—what you wish to accomplish in the allotted time. Unfortunately, many people are action oriented rather than goal oriented. They think only in terms of the immediate action that must be taken, rather than the results that are sought. A time-related goal is one that relates the importance of what has to be achieved to the corresponding work schedule.

Once these goals are clearly stated, plan your time so that you can give priority to the most important matters, the ones that will help you meet the goals. Whenever there is a conflict of what to do first, unless the urgency of the situation requires immediate action, the activity that leads to meeting your goals should get the highest priority.

Set Priorities and Stick to Them

Charles Schwab, the man whom Andrew Carnegie picked to manage Carnegie Steel, and who was selected to head the new Bethlehem Steel Company, was fond of telling the story of how he learned to manage time.

He consulted Ivy Lee, one of the pioneer management consultants. Some of his famous clients were J. P. Morgan, John D. Rockefeller, the DuPonts, and many giant corporations. Schwab told him: "I'm not managing now as well as I know how. What we need here is not more *knowing* but more *doing*. If you can give us something that will help us do the things we already know we ought to do, I'll gladly listen and pay you anything you ask."

"Fine," said Lee. "I can give you something right now that will increase your *action* and *doing* at least 50 percent." Lee asked Schwab to write the six most important tasks he had to do the next day and then to number them in order of importance. He then said: "When you come in tomorrow morning look at item number one and start working on it and don't start any other item until you have completed it. Then do the same with item two, and then item three, and so on until quitting time. Don't be concerned if you only finish two or three or even if you only finish one item. You'll be working on the most important ones. The others can wait. Spend the last five minutes of every working day making out a similar list for the next day. List the items you have not finished and add the new matters that have come up. Put them in priority order again. You may find that some new items are more important than items from the previous day's list that were not completed, and those previous day's items go back at the bottom of the list. If this continues to occur, it means that these matters were not important enough for you to do. They either should be dropped or delegated to another person.

"If after several days, you find that if you can't finish all the items by this method, you couldn't have with any other method either, and without some kind of system you probably wouldn't even have decided which were most important. After you have convinced yourself of the worth of this system, have all the members of your staff use the same system. Try it for as long as you want and then send me a check for what you think it was worth."

The whole interview lasted twenty-five minutes. In two weeks Schwab sent Lee a check for $25,000—a thousand dollars a minute. Schwab often told people that this lesson was the most profitable he had ever learned. Did it work? In five years Schwab turned his new company, Bethlehem Steel, into the biggest independent steel producer in the world, making Schwab a fortune of more than a hundred million dollars.

Make a Master List and Follow It
Follow Ivy Lee's advice: Set priorities and stick to them. This is the essential ingredient of effective time management. Use lists. Start by writing a master list on which you put down everything you

want to do. List them as they come to you. Importance is not considered. Rather than using loose papers, keep a notebook in which you can jot down every item you wish to accomplish.

Review the master list daily. Divide large projects into manageable components. Determine priorities. Which items should be done today; which can be deferred; which can be delegated. Develop a daily list for what you plan to do today and tentative lists for the balance of the week. Put on your calendar items that are deferred to later times.

Evaluate the daily lists in terms of the importance to meeting your goals. Schedule time for performing items on the list taking into consideration the urgency of the matter as well as how it will pay out in terms of value to your goals.

By conscientiously following this procedure, you will condition your subconscious mind to approach your daily activities in a time-oriented manner.

Know Your Energy Levels

Each person has levels of energy that vary over the day. Determine your periods of high energy. Some people work better in the morning; others later in the day. Some people work better right after eating; others are lethargic for an hour after lunch. Schedule difficult and complex tasks for high-energy times.

Keep a Time Journal

Do you know how you spend your time? Most people have only a vague concept of where the time goes. I have asked this question to countless people. Some had not given much thought to this but had an uncanny innate ability to utilize their time efficiently. On the other hand, some had set up time journals to record how they were spending their working hours.

You may question a busy person's ability to take time out to keep a time journal. Yes, it is tedious, and sometimes you can be so involved in an activity that it is neither feasible nor appropriate to stop and enter items in a journal. Realistically, in such a situation, you have to do your best to track your progress in the program, but if you miss recording a segment in your journal, write it up as soon thereafter as possible.

Keeping a time journal is not something you need to do forever. It should be done for at least three or four days each week for about two to three weeks to get a good sampling of how you spend your time. Then you can study the sheets and analyze just where most of your time is going.

Once you learn in what areas your time is wasted, you can take steps to correct them. Some are easily corrected; others are more complex.

Plagues That Steal Your Time

You had planned a full day's work. You had it all nicely scheduled. Now the day is over and only a fraction of what you had planned to accomplish has been done. Where did the time go?

Most likely you tackled the projects on your master list with full intent of completing them, but no sooner had you started than you were hit by one or more of the plagues that steal away our time. There are dozens of these time robbers. Review your time journal and you will see what are the most common time robbers that plague you and what we can do to minimize their effects.

Interruptions from Subordinates

Probably the most frequent interruptions are from one's own subordinates who have problems that they believe require your immediate attention. Most likely there are some people who interrupt you more often than others. They bring you every little problem rather than try to work out solutions themselves. One way to identify who these people are is to keep a record of these interruptions. Note the name of the person, the type of problem or question, and

how long it took to deal with it. By reviewing this record periodically, you will see who is taking your time and what problems they
are bringing to you.

Sometimes the problems that they bring you are important and
your advice, opinion, or orders are needed for them to continue the
work. But more often, they bring you matters that they should really deal with on their own.

Jack Welch, the brilliant CEO of General Electric, reported that
subordinates brought him problems that he believed they should
have solved on their own. He responded by asking them, "What do
you think should be done?" By throwing the problem back to
them, he forced them to think about it more. After a while his staff
members stopped coming to him unless his personal decision was
absolutely required. Follow Welch's practice. Tell your staff members that if they bring you a problem, they should also bring to you
at least one suggestion as to how it could be handled. In this way
they will have to think about it more thoroughly and will often
resolve the matter without interrupting you. And if they do have to
speak to you, the time they take will be much shorter.

The CEO of a Fortune 500 company told me that he became so
annoyed by constant interruptions from his staff with problems
and questions, he notified them that unless the situation was so
urgent that delay would cause irreparable damage, they should
hold their questions until five o'clock. Every day at that time he
opened his door to deal with these matters. It didn't take long for
his people to start trying to solve their own problems rather than
wait until the end of the day.

The Telephone

You're sitting at your desk deeply engrossed in your work and the
phone rings. It is a colleague with a business question. But does
this colleague get right down to business? Not usually. He or she
will chat about the weather, his weekend activities, her vacation

plans, before starting the business discussion. The time spent on most business calls could be shortened significantly if callers concentrated only on the business at hand. However, to eliminate all personal chitchat could have negative effects as well. A little social conversation smooths the relationships between people and helps develop a more pleasant work environment, resulting in more cooperation and teamwork.

Keep the social aspect of the conversation to a minimum. If the other person persists in lengthy unrelated discussions, politely say: "I'd love to hear more about that party, but I have a pile of papers here I have to get to right away," and then move into the business aspect of the conversation.

Keep calls brief. Plan the call before you pick up the telephone. List the key points you wish to cover and check them off as you reach them. One busy business executive usually starts the conversation with a comment that he has just five or ten minutes before leaving for a meeting and requests the other party to please keep the call brief. Where appropriate, send emails instead of phoning.

Visitors

If you work in a busy office, it is likely that other members of the staff will come in to talk with you. Most times these are business-related matters, but often they are just social visits. Such visits are nice, as they may break the monotony of the workday and sometimes help develop closer relations with other staff members, but they can be time-consuming.

Try to keep social visits to a minimum. If a colleague makes a practice of visiting you just to chat, diplomatically bring the visit to a close as rapidly as possible.

If an uninvited person calls on you, for example a sales rep, meet in the lobby instead of your office. Do not invite him or her into your office unless you are really interested in the product or service. Meetings in the lobby can be concluded in a few minutes. Once inside, it may take a lot longer to get rid of the sales rep. Another suggestion is to stand when talking to visitors who come into your office. Invite them to be seated only if you want them to stay.

Another way to minimize interruptions is to set aside one hour each morning as "privacy time." Put a "Do Not Disturb" sign on your door. Set your voice mail to take all calls. Let your staff know that that hour is private and unless there's a real emergency, you are not to be disturbed. Make sure your boss knows and approves, so he or she won't break into your private time. You'll be amazed how much you can accomplish in that hour.

Reserve Some Time for Yourself

All of us have lives outside of our jobs. We need time for families, our nonwork activities, and ourselves. Don't let your job overwhelm you.

Jeff Weinstein of Santa Monica, California, created the Counter, a successful fast-food chain, in which customers can custombuild their hamburgers. As the chain grew, he was working 24/7, with no time for himself and his family. He tried to set up a schedule and to budget his time. He tried not bringing work home. He tried to accomplish it all, but nothing worked, until he finally figured it out. He realized that if he could custom-build burgers, he could also custom-build his time.

The trick, he says, is being fluid, to move seamlessly from one area of life to another. His schedule includes starting his day by doing something for himself. He goes to the gym before work. He arrives at work later, but in a better mood, treating coworkers better, making them more productive. He accomplishes more and has more time to enjoy with his family.

One way to build in more time for yourself is to delegate more of the work you usually do to others. Analyze your workload. You will find that often you are doing work that subordinates are fully capable of doing. Even though you may truly enjoy that phase of the job, it is far more efficient to let others do it. Review Chapter 11 for suggestions on how to delegate effectively.

Don't Be Afraid to Say No

One of the most frequently heard complaints is that people feel overworked. "I am loaded down now—and the boss gives me another project. What can I do?" You don't have to accept every assignment. Quite often the boss may not be aware of all of the things you are working on. Speak up. Don't get upset or lose your temper. In a calm manner, explain just what you are working on and ask the boss to help you determine the priorities of each assignment. The boss may suggest you stop work on less important matters or may choose to give the new assignment to somebody else.

It is not only your boss who may ask you to do things you are too busy to do. You may be asked by a coworker for assistance. You may be asked to serve on a committee by a community organization in which you are a member. Before accepting or rejecting such requests, think carefully about the amount of time it would take. If you are truly too busy with higher priority matters, politely decline.

Be Patient

Managing time does not mean that things must be accomplished in a rush. Many real accomplishments are the result of long and patient efforts. Too many people lack patience. Everything cannot be accomplished immediately. "Can't wait" is characteristic of the century, and is written on everything; on commerce, on schools, on society, on churches.

SUM AND SUBSTANCE

- Make a master list in order of priority and stick to it.

- Schedule an hour of private time each day—time free of inter-ruptions and distractions. Use this time to review your sched-ule and adjust it to fit current priorities.

- Plan your day so you use your most energetic hours for tough matters and those hours when you are not at peak levels for lesser matters.

- Delegate. By delegating items of lesser import to others, you free yourself to deal with higher-level matters.

- Learn to say no. Know your time limitations and how to say no tactfully when it will help you reach your goals.

Chapter Seventeen

Selling Your Ideas

*Increase your sales by repeating this statement over and over again,
"My sales are improving every day; I am advancing, progressing, and
getting wealthier every day."*

In your job and in other aspects of your life, you often have to persuade people to accept your ideas. To succeed you must think like a salesperson. By studying and applying the techniques successful salespeople use, you will improve your capability to accomplish this.

Of the many elements that enter into scientific selling, none is more essential than that of persuasion. Salespeople often find a would-be customer's mind absolutely opposed to theirs. The customers do not want the merchandise, or at least think they do not, and are determined not to buy it. They brace themselves against all possibility of persuasion, of being influenced to do what they have decided not to do.

A little later, however, they cheerfully buy the article, pay for it, and feel sure they really want it. Their entire attitude has been changed by the art of persuasion, of winning over, which was all done by successive logical steps, each of which had to be taken in order or failure would have resulted.

You Can Learn to Be a Persuasive Person

Just as men and women are born with natural gifts for music and for art, so certain men and women have, in a high degree, the natural qualities that enable them to persuade others to their way of thinking.

While it is true that some people have more natural capacity at this than others, it is also true that most people can, by training, acquire the skills needed to succeed in persuasion. In addition, even if an untrained individual has natural talents in many areas, such as athletics, oratory, or commercial pursuits, people can be trained to become the equal of that individual.

Don't attribute a lost sale or a poor business decision to "hard luck." It is often caused by ignorance of the science of selling or management. Business is like a science, and almost any honest, dead-in-earnest, determined person can become an expert at it, if that person is willing to dedicate himself or herself.

Let's look at the one job where persuasiveness is a major element—selling. Even if you are not selling a product or a service, but are selling your ideas to other people, you must think of yourself as a salesperson.

To find out whether you have persuasive ability, you must analyze your talent. In this matter, however, it should be borne in mind that human nature, especially in youth, is plastic, and that we can be molded by others, or we can mold ourselves.

Even if you do not have a decided talent for selling, it can be acquired. By proper training in selling, which means the right kind of reading, observing, listening, and practicing, you can develop your ability and become a good salesperson.

Get the Other Person's Attention

In order to persuade another person to buy your product or service or to accept your ideas, you must first get their full attention; otherwise nothing you say will even be listened to. It is often a difficult matter—to get the attention of someone who at the least is not interested in what you have to say and at the most may be braced against you. But it is absolutely necessary, before you can persuade anybody to do what you want done, to secure that person's attention.

When dealing with a person you work with, you can get his or her attention by commenting about something you know will be of interest to him or her. It is not necessary to speak of trivial or extraneous matters to attract that person's attention. A direct question or comment on the situation involved is a good first step.

For example, if you wish to persuade a colleague to serve on a committee to evaluate a new piece of equipment, a comment about the frequent breakdown of current equipment would surely get attention.

Sometimes you must take dramatic steps to get the attention of people who are reluctant to accept what you are selling. In the early 1990s Continental Airlines ranked last in customer service among the ten largest airlines. Bureaucracy was stifling everything, from determining the color of pencils used on boarding passes to how a form should be folded. Obeying these rules, as specified in the rule book—there actually was one—was considered more important than making creative decisions. There was no time to waste. In order to get the idea across that the rule book was being done away with for all time, CEO Gordon Bethune took a group of employees into the parking lot. He threw the rule book into a fifty-gallon drum, doused it with gasoline, and set it afire. Word spread . . . like wildfire . . . and Continental was on its way to rebuilding employee morale and success.

Getting attention need not be this dramatic. Sometimes asking a key question will do the trick. By phrasing the question in a way that suggests you may have a solution to a problem, you are sure to get the attention of the other party. When Darlene D. wanted to sell her boss on instituting a flexible hours program in her department, she approached her boss with this question: "Dave, I know how concerned you are with the lower productivity we have been experiencing. One of the causes of this is our difficulty in recruiting good clerical workers. If there was a way to attract more skilled people, you would want to know about it, wouldn't you?" The only response Dave could give was "Yes." She now had his attention and was able to present her arguments for considering her suggestions.

Another way of gaining attention is to be creative. Natalie Carson, head of women's apparel for TravelSmith, a travel outfitting business, got her boss's attention by reporting, "Ask any woman what she believes is the single essential item in every woman's closet. She'll most likely say, 'A little black dress.'" Scott Sklar, co-CEO of TravelSmith, didn't think dresses belonged in his catalog. Ms. Carlson thought otherwise. Carlson spent long weekends in Paris—her husband worked there—and she knew she was right. So she went on the hunt for the perfect black knit wrinkle-free dress that would make *her* feel at home among the stylish women at dinner parties. Unable to find one, she designed and developed her own perfect little black travel dress, and demonstrated that it clearly solved the problem. Sklar listened, and was persuaded. Result: The little black wrinkle-free travel dress has been the number one product in the catalog ever since. This led to Natalie Carlson's promotion to vice president of merchandising.

Arouse Desire

Once you gain attention, the next step is to get the person to be thoroughly interested in your proposition. You must arouse the desire to embrace the idea you are proposing. Once this is accomplished, acceptance is almost certain. To do this you must appeal to the emotions—to the heart rather than to the head.

You will never arouse a person's desire by talking about what you want. First, you must explore what the other person really wants. What is important to that person? What turns him or her on? To do this you must truly listen to what that person says in answer to your questions. Listen carefully. Be prepared to pick up subtleties that can lead you to that person's real interest. Then by adapting your comments to fit into that person's desires, you are on the way to winning your point.

I was talking recently with some friends about the rapid rise of a young salesman that surprised everybody who knew him. One of my friends said that the whole secret was his marvelous power to persuade people to change their minds, to make a prospect see things from his point of view. He said he had never before met another person who had such remarkable success in changing another's mind to his way of thinking. "And this," he added, "is the essence, the quintessence, if you will, of selling—the power to make another see things as we see them."

How did he do this? He sought and found what was in the heart of his prospect. What was the one thing that would really affect that prospect's thinking? By listening intently, observing facial expressions and body language, he targeted the key factor. "Most often," he told me, "it was an emotional rather than a practical factor."

The best and most successful teachers are not always the most learned, but those who get hold of the hearts of their pupils, those who possess kindness, personal interest, and sympathy, qualities which, apart from scholarship, make the best teachers. These same qualities give all of us the basic ingredients to be persuasive people.

While education and intelligence are indispensable, it is not so much smartness, as the warm human heart qualities that make a person popular and successful.

Be Sincere

Some people have sort of a hypnotic power that passes for persuasiveness, and enables them to get what they want at the outset, but
it is not based on honesty, and in the long run seriously hurts the
business. An example of this is the magnetic, spellbinding sales rep
who will often bring in larger orders than some other sales reps,
but in the end will lose customers and injure the reputation of the
company. Better is the one who does not sell nearly as much to
start with, but will make many more friends, and will hold customers, because he or she looks out for their interest and only
tries to sell them what it is to their advantage to buy. By studying
their needs, and winning their confidence and goodwill, this sales
rep establishes a long-term profitable relationship. The ability to
make others think as you do is a tremendous power, and carries
great responsibility. If it is not kindly and honestly used, it will
prove a boomerang and injure most the one who uses it. Such
people will soon become known as "spellbinders" and will turn
people off.

Today it is the clean, straight-from-the-shoulder cold-facts talk
that most people want. Yet people of persuasive powers can present those facts in such a way that the prospect will be made to feel
that the presenter is a friend and acting entirely in the prospect's
interest. No one relishes the idea of being "managed," and no matter how much the other person loves flattery, your motives will be
questioned if you attempt it.

Very tactful and honest praise, however, will help your cause
considerably. Remember that the person with whom you are dealing will always be on guard against any sort of deceit and will be
looking for evidence of insincerity. Nobody wants to be duped or
lulled into surrender. Above all, remember that there is no substitute for sincerity in any field.

Consider the Other Person's Interests

There is nothing that will take the place in our lives of absolute transparency, simplicity, honesty, and kindness. The Golden Rule is the only rule of conduct that will bring true success in any business.

When you are in doubt as to how your acts will affect another, just ask yourself this question: "Would I like to have someone else do this to me?"

Nathan Straus, an early co-owner of Macy's department store and noted philanthropist, when asked what had contributed most to the success of his remarkable career, replied, "I always looked out for the person at the other end of the bargain." He said that if he got a bad bargain himself he could stand it, even if his losses were heavy, but he could never afford to have the person who dealt with him get a bad bargain. By always looking at the transaction from the point of view of the other parties involved, Straus placed the focus on what the other parties perceived was their best interest.

Measure the Other Person

An important step in becoming a persuasive person is to make a study of the power of penetration, of character-reading ability. Make it your business to study people and the motives that actuate them.

Expertise in reading human nature is just as valuable a tool in persuasion as expertise in litigation is to a lawyer, or as skill in diagnosis is to a physician. People who can read human nature, who can "size up" others quickly, who can arrive at an accurate estimate of character, no matter what their vocation or profession, have a great advantage over others.

The ability to look deeply into others' nature is a cultivatable quality, and we have a great opportunity to study this when we deal with multitudes of people. It is an education in itself to form the habit of measuring, weighing, estimating the different people we meet, for in this way we are improving our own powers of observation, sharpening our perceptive faculties, improving our judgment.

Successful men and women attribute their career advancement to this understanding of others' mentality and motivation. It has enabled them to deal more effectively with their bosses, their subordinates, their coworkers, customers, vendors, and the public.

No two mentalities are exactly alike, and you must approach each one through the avenue of the least resistance. Learn the other person's personal interests. If a person is passionately fond of music or crazy about golf or is a connoisseur of art, this may give you a hint as to the right line of approach.

Top salespeople make a practice of carefully ferreting out the interests, hobbies, and special concerns of prospects, such as sports teams the prospect favors, the ages of their children, and similar details, and integrate their findings into their sales presentations. This works equally well when dealing with those people in the organization with whom you must develop good relationships in order to move up the career ladder.

Do not be hasty in your judgment or make up your mind too quickly in sizing up people. Hold your decision in abeyance until you have read off the character hieroglyphics written on the face and person, and in the manner, for all these are significant, and each means something. In other words, read all a person's earmarks or character labels, get in all the evidence you can instead of acting on your first quick impression, because a great deal depends on the accuracy of your judgment. Reread the discussion of body language in Chapter 14.

The face is a bulletin board; it is a program of the performance going on inside, and the important thing is to learn to read it quickly and accurately. The facial expressions, the attitude, the manner, the language, the look in the eye are letters of the character alphabet that spell out an individual's personality.

Everything that is natural, spontaneous, unpremeditated, is indicative of certain qualities a person possesses; and if that person is putting on, or is posing, you can pierce the mask of pretense and discount it.

Learn About Their Lives

It is easier to persuade people you know to go along with you than it is to persuade a stranger. One of the keys to persuasion is to point out how what it is you want someone to do will be of value to that person. With strangers—such as sales prospects—it is not always easy to learn what is important to them. But with people you work with or know well, you should already know their feelings, desires, and attitudes.

Keep in mind that people are different and what persuades one person may not have any influence on another. Get to know your employees, colleagues, the people outside of your department and company with whom you deal as individual human beings. Each one of the people with whom you work has a life outside the job that is usually more important to that person than the job itself. By talking to your coworkers about the things that really concern them outside the job, you let them know you are interested in them as people—not just workers.

Talking to them is only the beginning. It is not necessary to pry into their private lives, but by listening to them—empathizing with them, observing their reactions—you can learn a great deal about how they feel, what they really are like, and what motivates them.

Diplomacy and Tact Lead to Effective Persuasion

Tact is one of the greatest aids to success in life. Many prominent business executives report that tact heads the list in their success recipe, the other three things being personality, enthusiasm, and knowledge of business.

Tact enables you to pass sentinels, gates, and bars, gain an entrance to the very sanctum where the tactless person never enters. Tact gets a hearing where genius cannot; it is admitted when talent is denied; it is listened to when ability without tact cannot get a hearing.

Alex was a brilliant engineer. His expertise in computer science was unsurpassed. Although his presentations to management were technically impeccable, he antagonized his listeners with his arrogance. As one manager commented, "When he answers my questions, he makes me feel stupid for asking them." When he was criticized for his lack of tact, he responded, "Too bad, they are too dense to understand me."

After being passed over several times for promotion, Alex was persuaded to see an executive coach. It took weeks for Alex to overcome his tendency to push his ideas on others rather than to sell them. Through exercises and meditations, he was able to train his subconscious mind to accept that his superior knowledge alone was not enough to gain him the advancement in his career he craved. This resulted in his accepting other people's weak spots and looking for their strengths instead of scoffing at their limitations. Over time, Alex changed his approach in his interpersonal relationships, and made presentations with more tact and consideration of others' feelings, resulting in his achieving his career goals.

Overcoming Objections and Closing the Sale

When you present your ideas to others, there are likely to be some aspects of your concepts to which they may take exception. Look at this as a challenge, not a problem. Salespeople like objections. It helps them determine what the prospect really wants and enables them to face up to that and increase their chances of making the sale. Good salespeople anticipate what objections are likely to be presented and are prepared to counteract them. You should do the same.

If you wish to persuade others to accept a concept, study all of the negative aspects that may be brought up by others and be prepared to rebut them or, if they are valid, to show how the advantages of your concept outweigh the disadvantages. Prepare facts and figures to substantiate your position—but also think of the intangible aspects and appeal to others' emotions. Just as the close—the final acceptance—is the culmination of the sale for a sales rep, the acceptance of what you have sought to persuade others of is the result you aim for.

Once you have dealt with all the objections, you are ready to make the close. Before taking this final step, give yourself a brief pep talk: "I know this is a sound idea and will be of great value to the organization. I am prepared to do all I can to convince my boss to accept it." This will activate your subconscious mind to reinforce your confidence that you will succeed. Then push forward with your closing step.

One of the most effective approaches to sell an idea to another person is to ask that person to participate in evaluating the concept. Divide a paper into two columns. Head one "Negatives" and the other "Positives." Immediately list the major objections that have been brought up in the "negative" column and write the counteracting arguments in the "positive" column. Add to the "positive" column all of the additional benefits that have been discussed. If you have done your homework, you should have many more positives than negatives. Then state: "Let's look at some of the reasons that may cause you to hesitate to accept this idea and weigh them against the reasons in favor of going ahead. In your opinion, which weighs heavier?" The answer has to be on the positive side.

Once you have obtained agreement that your concept is viable, say, "Inasmuch as you agree that this is a good idea, I would like to discuss the next step in implementing it."

If the concept has to be sold to your boss's boss or to other executives before it can be adopted, suggest that you will be happy to assist in that presentation.

By carefully preparing and by following the approaches used by successful salespeople, you can present and sell your ideas to others and get the great satisfaction from seeing your concepts accepted and carried out.

SUM AND SUBSTANCE

- In your job and in other aspects of your life, you often have to persuade people to accept your ideas. To succeed you must think like a salesperson.

- In order to persuade another person to buy your product or service or to accept your ideas, you must first get that person's full attention; otherwise nothing you say will even be listened to.

- You must arouse the desire to possess the thing you have for sale, or to embrace the idea you are proposing. Once this is accomplished, acceptance is almost certain. To do this you must appeal to the emotions—to the heart rather than to the head.

- No matter how intelligent or competent you may be, your advancement in your career depends on developing good relationships with other people—your bosses, your coworkers, your subordinates, your customers, and others with whom you must interact.

- Keep in mind that people are different and what persuades one may not have any influence on another. Get to know your employees, colleagues, the people outside of your department and company with whom you deal as individual human beings.

- If you wish to persuade others to accept a concept, study all of the negative aspects that may be brought up by others and be prepared to rebut them or, if they are valid, to show how the advantages of your concept outweigh the disadvantages.

- Before taking your final step, give yourself a pep talk. This will activate your subconscious mind to reinforce your confidence that you will succeed.

Chapter Eighteen

Advancing Your Career

The only way to climb is to keep your eye fixed on your star. Visualize the thing you want to be; keep it in your mind constantly and work for it with all your might. The important thing is always to have a driving motive back of your work, an inspiring goal ahead, something big, something grand to look forward to, something that will stimulate your ambition, which will satisfy your aspiration.

Do you want to be greater than you are? Do you want to be grander or nobler? Then you must be willing to give up fear, grudges, peeves, and self-condemnation. You must give to get. You must give up negative thinking in order to practice constructive thinking. You must love the person you want to be. You must give up the person you now are. You must be willing to let go of the old so that you might experience the new.

You can fall in love with music, you can fall in love with art, and you can fall in love with the law. You can sit down and contemplate health, happiness, peace of mind, abundance, security, right action, harmony, inspiration, and guidance. You can contemplate a career which will not only give you financial reward, but also provide the joy and satisfaction of doing something you love and something that is worthwhile. You can dwell on these things, give them your attention, devotion, loyalty. You, too, can become entranced, fascinated, absorbed, and engrossed; and the law of your subconscious will respond. As you think in your heart or subconscious, so are you. So will you act, and so will you become.

It is not as you think in your head, but in your heart, because these ideas have to be emotionalized and felt as true. Any thought, any idea, that you dwell upon induces and evokes a certain emotional response. When you continue to do that, it sinks into and impregnates your subconscious and becomes compulsive; therefore, you are compelled to be, to do, and to express that which you meditated on.

If your ambition is not thoroughly alive, if it is spasmodic, if it tends to sag, especially under discouragement, you should build it up, strengthen it in every possible way. For instance, if you are in a business firm, make up your mind to be a big business executive; prepare yourself for a partnership in your employer's firm. This is a perfectly legitimate ambition that has been realized by many people who began at the bottom of the ladder. Then the very thought of sometime seeing your name over the door of the establishment in which you are now a clerk will give you a tremendous object to work for; and whether your name ever appears over that particular door or not does not matter so much, for you will get the training, the preparation for something else just as good or better. Whatever happens, the ambition and the preparation for partnership will be the best possible developers for you.

Larry W. is a man who has won a great name and place for himself in the business world, who has made it a practice from boyhood to set a pace for his ambition by daily heart-to-heart talks with himself, by constantly "jacking" himself up, as he calls it, to his highest level.

Larry is convinced that much of his accomplishment is due to his early formed habit of relentlessly keeping after himself, urging himself continually to do the biggest thing possible for him. He says that if he did not keep right after his ambition, if he did not constantly prod it and set a pace for himself, in a very few months his standards would drop, his energy lag, his ideals sag, and his whole life deteriorate.

Three Steps to Success

The vital first step to success is to find out the thing you love to do, and then do it. Unless you love your work, you cannot possibly consider yourself successful at it, even if all the rest of the world hails you as a great success. Loving your work, you have a deep desire to carry it out. If you are drawn to become a psychiatrist, it is not enough to get a diploma and hang it on the wall. You will want to keep up with the field, attend conventions, and continue studying the mind and its workings. You will visit other clinics and pore over the latest scientific journals. In other words, you will work to keep yourself informed of the most advanced methods of alleviating human suffering, because you put the interests of your patients first.

But what if, as you read these words, you find yourself thinking, "I can't take the first step, because I don't know what it is I want to do. How on earth do I find a field of effort that I will love?" If that is your situation, pray for guidance in this way:

"The Infinite Intelligence of my subconscious mind reveals to me my true place in life."

Repeat this phrase quietly, positively, and lovingly to your deeper mind. As you persist with faith and confidence, the answer will come to you as a feeling, a hunch, or a tendency in a certain direction. It will come to you clearly and in peace, and as an inner silent awareness.

The second step to success is to specialize in some particular branch of work and strive to excel in it. Suppose you choose chemistry as a profession. You should concentrate on one of the many branches in this field and give all your time and attention to your chosen specialty. Your enthusiasm should make you want to know all there is available about this field. You should become ardently interested in this work and should desire to use it to serve the world.

The third step is the most important one. You must be sure that the thing you want to do does not contribute only to your own success. Your desire must not be selfish. It must benefit humanity. The path of a complete circuit must be formed. In other words, your idea must go forth with the purpose of blessing or serving the world. It will then come back to you magnified and full of blessings. If you work only for your own benefit, you do not complete this essential circuit. You may appear to be successful, but the short-circuit you have generated in your life may lead over time to limitation or sickness.

In considering the three steps to success, you must never forget the underlying power of the creative forces of your subconscious mind. This is the energy behind all the steps in any plan of success. Your thought is creative. Thought fused with feeling becomes a subjective faith or belief.

Using the Subconscious Mind to Get Ahead
Johann Wolfgang von Goethe, the great German poet, used his imagination wisely when confronted with difficulties and predicaments. According to Goethe's biographers, he was accustomed to filling many hours quietly holding imaginary conversations. He would imagine one of his friends sitting across from him. He imagined his friend giving him the right or appropriate answers to his questions accompanied with his usual gestures and tonal qualities of the voice. He made the entire imaginary scene as real and as vivid as possible.

When Geri P., a young financial advisor, read about this, she determined to adopt the technique of Goethe. She began to have imaginary conversations with a multimillionaire investor whom she knew and who had once congratulated her on her wise and sound judgment in recommending investments. She dramatized this imaginary conversation until she had psychologically fixed it as a form of belief in her subconscious mind.

Geri's inner talking and controlled imagination certainly agreed with her aim, which was to make sound investments for her clients, to make money for them, and to see them prosper financially from her wise counsel. She is still using her subconscious mind in her business, and she is a brilliant success in her field.

Make Good Decisions

Probably the most significant characteristic of successful people is their ability to make decisions—promptly and accurately—and their capacity to implement those decisions and follow through to assure that the decisions result in satisfactory resolutions to the problems involved.

In my many years listening to men and women who beg me to help them overcome failure, I've found that one common trait they all share is their wishy-washy approach to decision making. When faced with solving a problem, they procrastinate and are overly cautious. And once the decision is made, they do not follow through.

One of the greatest gifts God has bestowed on humans is the power of free choice—the power to analyze problems, make decisions regarding their solution, and put them into effect.

Tommy F. was faced with a major career decision. He had to decide whether or not to seek a new job. Although he loved his present job, he was not making enough money and as the business was not doing well, there was little chance he could get a raise in pay. A competitor offered him a job that would pay a bit more than he was making and appeared to have good opportunity for advancement. The competitor wanted an immediate answer, but Tommy prevailed upon him to wait for a decision until the following Friday. It was a good offer and he needed the additional money. However, he was concerned that going to the competitor wasn't fair to his current employer, who had trained him and helped him acquire the skills he had in his work. He prayed over it and then dismissed it from his mind, knowing that his subconscious mind would make the right decision.

Sure enough, on Wednesday, his boss called him in and told him that they had just closed a lucrative contract and he was putting him in charge of it with a managerial title and a good pay raise.

Tommy was convinced that it was God's will that he stay with his company and that his subconscious mind kept him from accepting the other offer immediately so he could receive the promotion.

Be Fair to Yourself

Lisa F. believed she was ready for promotion and advancement, yet she resented her supervisor. She felt that this woman was blocking her movement up. She discussed this with an older and wiser friend, who explained that she was unjust to herself, placing this woman on a pedestal, making her greater than the Infinite within her. This attitude makes no sense. By assuming that the supervisor was greater than the Infinite, she was denying the power of the Infinite, which is omnipotent and all-powerful.

Lisa made things equal by affirming, "Promotion is mine; advancement is mine; achievement is mine through the power of the Infinite." In time in her subconscious mind she rejected the notion that her supervisor was to blame for her failure to be promoted. Instead she marshaled her strength to improve her own work and attitude, which eventually led to the promotion she desired.

What you feel, you attract, and what you imagine, you become.

You can imagine yourself as a bum; you can imagine yourself jumping trains as a hobo. Keep it up and you'll become a hobo. But you can also imagine that you are a tremendous success, that you're a great actor; you can imagine yourself before an audience, making them laugh and cry, realizing the power within you to bring the beauty of Shakespeare to enrich the lives of your listeners.

Some people say that they can't get ahead, can't get promoted because they are working in a place where there is no opportunity for advancement or where wages are set by rigid standards. All this is not necessarily true. You can use the laws of mind to advance and to move forward. The secret is to love what you are doing now; to do the best you can where you are. Be cordial, kind, affable, and full of goodwill. Think big and think of riches, and your present work will simply be a stepping-stone to your triumph. Be conscious of your true worth, and claim riches in your mind, for yourself and for every single person you meet during the day, whether it be your boss, an associate, the foreman, a customer, or a friend—all those around you. You will feel your radiation of riches and advancement, and it will very soon open up a new door of opportunity for you.

People are constantly asking, "How can I get ahead in life, improve my circumstances, get a raise in salary, buy a new car and a new home, and have all the money I need in order to do what I have to do when I want to do it?"

The answer to all of these questions comes through learning to use the laws of your own mind: the law of cause and effect, the law of increase, and the law of attraction; these laws of your mind work with the same precision and exactitude as do the laws of physics, chemistry, and mathematics—and as definitely as the law of gravity.

Become Visible

You can't depend on your immediate boss alone to assure your advancement. Josh K. was a good worker. Ken, his boss, often complimented him on his work and often commented that he would recommend Josh to be promoted into his job when he retired. Unfortunately, Ken died suddenly—and the company brought in an outsider to head the department. Josh was not even considered. Why? Nobody at the higher levels in the organization even knew Josh. He was invisible. In many organizations there are many highly competent people who, like Josh, will never make much progress because nobody knows who they are. In order to move up in your career, you must be visible not only to your boss, but to other managers as well.

Five Ways to Become Visible

It's not necessary to hire a public relations consultant to let other people know how competent, bright, creative, and capable you are. Here are five simple steps you can take to make sure other people in your organization know you:

1. *Speak up.* Participate in meetings you attend. Don't just sit there. Don't be afraid to express your ideas and make suggestions. Caution: Prepare for the meeting by reviewing the agenda and be sure of your facts and the ramifications of any suggestions you make.

2. *Help others by providing them with information in their areas.* Valerie P. made a practice of clipping articles from trade journals and sending them to coworkers or managers who she knew would be interested in them. She developed a reputation of being a person who was alert to other people's interests, and this was a significant factor in her advancement in the company.

3. *Volunteer.* Take on assignments that may be avoided by others. Bill M. volunteered to chair the company's annual fund-raising drive for the United Way. In this assignment he visited every department in the organization and became

known to most of the department managers. A few months later, a manager who was expanding his operation offered Bill a challenging and remunerative position on his new team.

4. *Become active in professional organizations.* Darlene A. worked in the marketing department of a top-level consumer products firm. There were several other young marketing specialists in her department—all competing for advancement. Her competitors were all bright and creative and, like Darlene, graduates of the best schools. Darlene had to do something to stand out.

As a member of the local chapter of the American Marketing Association, she agreed to serve on the Program Committee. Her first assignment was to find a speaker for the April meeting. Her choice—the vice president of marketing of her company. Although Darlene had never spoken to this executive and was certain he did not even know who she was, she invited him. He not only agreed, but also told her it was quite an honor to be invited. On two occasions prior to the meeting he met with Darlene to discuss the talk. At the meeting, Darlene sat next to him on the dais and introduced him. From that time on Darlene was visible to the vice president and began to move rapidly ahead of her competitors.

5. *Write an article.* Most trade publications welcome articles from people in the field discussing various aspects of their work. Having a published article gives the writer visibility—not only in his or her own organization, but also to other firms in the field. As advancement in your career often requires a job change, this not only adds to your credentials, but also brings you to the attention of managers in other

companies and executive recruiters. Caution: Before submitting an article on any aspect of your current job, always get permission from the appropriate authority in your company to avoid violations of proprietary information or legal complications.

Change Course

There are times when you are stymied in your job and in order to get ahead it is necessary to find a new position either in your current firm or outside. You may have to take a few steps backward so that you can move forward.

Some business leaders don't have to be forced to change course. Intuitively they know the value of doing so periodically. Ellen Kullman, a top DuPont executive, left a large, powerful job in one division of DuPont to create a new safety products division for the company. This seemed like a big step down, since she had left a top position to head a start-up with no assets and only thirty employees. Half of her colleagues at DuPont thought she had done something wrong to be demoted, and the other half thought she was "just nuts." But in spite of the doubts and negativity around her, she knew she had been right when that start-up evolved into a $5.5 billion business. Kullman's advice to others who face resistance when they make difficult decisions rather than stagnate: "Continue to reinvent."

Earlier in her career, Liz Smith, who later became president of Avon Products, was running Kraft Foods' giant Jell-O brand when she chose to transfer instead to a small U.S. import business related to a new European acquisition. She says everybody thought she was crazy, but she knew she wanted experience in sales and global distribution, and by doing the unexpected and not being swayed by criticism, she got what she needed.

Success means to increase our capacities and abilities along all lines and in every direction so that we release our inner powers. The promotion, the money, and the contacts we make are the images or likenesses, as well as the physical forms, of the states of mind that produce them.

Life is addition. Add to your wealth, power, wisdom, knowledge, and faith by studying the law of your conscious and subconscious mind. Affirm, "My good is flowing to me now, ceaselessly, tirelessly, joyously, and copiously," and God's riches will flow into your receptive, open mind.

SUM AND SUBSTANCE

- The vital first step to success is to find out the thing you love to do, and then do it. Unless you love your work, you cannot possibly consider yourself successful at it, even if all the rest of the world hails you as a great success.

- Those who fear to make decisions or are afraid to make choices are actually refusing to recognize their own divinity.

- Never stop learning. Keeping up with the latest developments in your field is one way to assure long-term success in your career.

- Begin now to repeat the word "success" to yourself with faith and conviction. Your subconscious mind will accept it as true of you, and you will be under a subconscious compulsion to succeed.

- Do the best you can where you are. Be cordial, kind, affable, and full of goodwill. Be conscious of your true worth, and claim riches in your mind for yourself and for every single person you meet during the day, whether it be your boss, an associate, a customer, or a friend—all those around you. You will feel your radiation of riches and advancement, and it will very soon open up a new door of opportunity for you.

- Become visible. Make sure that the decision makers in your organization know your capabilities and availability. Review the five steps to becoming visible listed above.

Index

AA. *See* Alcoholics Anonymous
Ability, responsibility and, 133
Acceptance vs. punishment, 23–24
Accomplishments. *See also*
    Achievement(s)
    inventory of, 10–11
    mind, 9, 28
    praise for, 159
Achievement(s), 62
    enthusiasm leading to, 56–57
    focus on, 20
    of goals, 5–6, 32–33
    publicizing, 155
    secret of, 75–76
    self-reliance and, 34–35
    Success File and, 156–57
Action oriented vs. goal oriented, 189
Adaptability, 59–60, 62
Adaptation, problem solving with, 102
Advancement. *See* Achievement(s)
Adversity, overcoming, 61–62, 87
Advice, 155
Affirmation, 27
A&G Merchandising Company, 158
Ahrendts, Angela, 65–66
Alcoholics Anonymous, 14, 117

Allen, Fred, 103–4
Almighty, 72
Ambition
    arousing, 67–68
    leadership and, 127–28
    mediocrity vs., 34–35
    strengthening, 212
American Express, 126–27
Anger, 173–74
Anxiety, 71
Appearance, personality traits and,
    41–42
Appreciation
    building collaboration with, 149
    expressing, 148–49, 157, 158
    failing to express, 150–51
    personal letter of, 150, 156
    sincere gratitude and, 151–52
Article publishing, for visibility,
    219–20
Ash, Mary Kay, 127–28, 155
Athlete, adversity and, 87
Attention, 202, 209
    asking question to get, 200–201
    creativity and, 201
    persuasion and, 200–201

Attitude
  change and, 63
  enthusiasm and, 56
  as ethical code, 138
  kindly, 44
  mental, 8–9, 43
  optimistic, 9, 28, 29–30, 37, 77
Attraction, Law of, 216, 217
  applying, 42–43, 45–46, 94
  implementing, 49–50
  learning, 40
  mastering, 39
Attributes, for success, 1, 15–16
Audience, understanding, 162–63, 171–72
Aura, 46
Averages, law of, 175
Award, 150, 155, 156

Bankruptcy, 30–31, 64, 65
Beethoven, Ludwig von, 4, 56, 85
Behavior, 152
Belief(s)
  changing, 78
  character and, 35
  enthusiasm and, 56
  in failure, 17
  false, 80, 81
  health and, 74
  in leadership ability, 130–31
  receiving and, 94
  relaxation and, 77
  about self, 17–18, 26, 80, 124
  subconscious mind and, 134
Bethlehem Steel Company, 189–90
Bethune, Gordon, 200
Blue Monday, 37
Blues, beating, 78–79
Body ailments, 73–74
Body language, 172
Bounce back, from failure, 68–69
Burberry, 65, 66
Buyer, in fashion field, 6

Candor, 46
Career
  advancement, key ingredient of,
    205, 211

changing course and, 220–21
  control of, 37
  dream vs. satisfying, 9–10
  goals, 5, 142, 143
  limitations on women, 5
  success and, 1, 119
  visibility and, 217–18
Carnegie Steel, 189
Carson, Natalie, 201
Catastrophe, 36
Cause and effect, law of, 217
Chambers, John, 22–23
Change
  attitude, 63
  course, for career, 220–21
  fear of, 65, 69
  habit, 116
  resisting, 59, 142
  subconscious mind accepting, 144
  from supervisor to team leader,
    143–44
  welcoming, to reduce stress, 81
Character, as destiny, 35
Character-reading ability, success and,
    204
Charm, personal, 41
Chenault, Kenneth, 126–27
Christianity, 4, 5
Chrysler Corporation, 65
CISCO, 22–23
Claiborne, Liz, 66
Closing the sale, 208–9
Coaching, 21–22, 116
Collaboration
  advantages of, 169
  building with appreciation, 149
  enthusiasm and, 145–46
  on job, 144–45
  organizations and, 135
Comfort zone vs. change, 142
Commitments
  accepting important, 81
  in face of obstacles, 133
  participation in decisions and, 145
  strengthening, 113
  to success, 127–28
  team and, 135, 146

Communication
  delegation and, 129–30
  effective, 160, 171–72
  empathy and, 167
  engineers vs. bankers, 163
  on job, 162
  sending and receiving, 171–72
  team leader and, 137
Competency, 26
Competition, 32
Computer graphics, retraining in,
  74–75
Concentration, 75–76, 77
Conceptive realm, 75, 79
Conceptual realm. See Conceptive realm
Confidence, 25. See also Self-esteem
Conflict resolution, team and, 140
Conscious mind. See also Subconscious
  mind
  architect of city and, 97
  clearing, to solve problems, 79
  feeding positive thought into, 75–76,
    144
  influencing character and, 131–32
  law of, 221
  manifesting from subconscious, 84
  as pen for subconscious, 174–75
  taking charge of, 88
  words of truth and, 72
Contemplation, relaxation and, 74
Continental Airlines, 200
Control point, 129
Cooperation, 119, 140
Cordiality, practice of, 47–48
Counseling, 116, 180–81
The Counter, 195
Courage, test of, 87, 89–90
Coworker, dealing with unhappy,
  183–84
Creative principle, language and,
  27–28
Creativity, 65
  getting attention and, 201
  honing, 100–102, 105
  imagination and, 93–94, 97–98
  to reduce stress, 81
  revives dying enterprise, 103–4

  stimulating, 102–3
  of subconscious mind, 33, 93
  vision and, 104
Criticism
  accepting as constructive, 77
  compliments vs., 153–54
  correcting behavior vs., 152, 158
  questions vs., 170–71
  reinforcing poor behavior and, 152
  self-condemnation and, 174

Darkness, light as antidote to, 78–79
Decision-making, 216
  fear and, 221
  leadership and, 125–26
  ownership of, 145
  successful people and, 215
Defeat, invincible through, 90–91
Defensiveness vs. positive approach, 29
Delegation, 197
  communication, authority and,
    129–30
  as requirement for success, 128, 134
  workload and, 195–96
Depression, 78–79
Desire, 7–8, 209
  arousing, to embrace idea, 201–2
  to benefit humanity, 214
  God and, 72
  listening and, 202
Determination, 66
  brains vs., 5
  desire and, 7–8
  enthusiasm and, 54–55, 57
Diplomacy, effective persuasion and,
  206–7
Disagreement, 170–71
Disappointment, goals and, 4
Disposition, maintaining cheerful,
  43–44
Divine, 75
Doubt
  erasing from vocabulary, 133
  faith vs., 25–26, 84
  fatal to achievement, 75
Douglass, Frederick, 19–20
Dreams, 4–7, 9–10

DuPont Corporation, 220
Dyslexia, overcoming, 23

EAP. *See* Employee Assistance Program
Edison, Thomas, 4, 60, 65, 99, 104
Elimination, of paperwork, 101–2
Emotions, 209
  affirmative, 25
  appealing to, 202
  controlling dark, 54
  idea and subconscious mind, 115
  negative, 26, 31, 57–58, 64
  range of, 40
  thought and, 174
  victim of, 79
Empathy, 43, 49
  as listening skill, 167
  unhappy coworker and, 185–86
  using, to find other's motivation,
    206
Employee Assistance Program,
    179–81, 186
Encouragement
  discovering self and, 68
  of ideas, 168–69
  through praise, 155
  of team members, 141
Enthusiasm, 49
  achievements and, 56–57
  attracting business and, 52–53
  determination and, 54–55, 57
  enhancing collaboration, 145–46
  Infinite Power and, 51
  work and, 52–53, 55, 56, 57
Environment, self-development and, 68,
    69–70
Equanimity, 63, 64, 76, 92
Evaluation, self, 9
Executives, supporting change, 143
Expectancy, 7–8, 9
Eye contact, as skill for listening, 166

Facial expressions, 166, 205–6
Faculties, cultivation of, 66
Failure, 9, 70
  as belief, 17
  bouncing back and, 68–69

communication as determiner of
    success or, 160
dealing constructively with, 63–64
in early life, 16
fear of, 59–60, 82
learning from, 60, 67
as life script, 18–19
loss of self-esteem from, 184, 185
as negative thinking, 33
procrastination and, 110, 111
reversing, 17
unconquered spirit vs., 90
Faith
  in ability, 133, 141
  as antidote to fear, 84–85, 91
  doubt vs., 25–26, 84
  Infinite Spirit and, 74
  leadership and, 126
  as optimist, 91
Farmer, 61–62
Fate, 37, 133
Fear, 83, 87, 88–89
  attracting what is dreaded and, 83, 91
  as cause of misery on job, 83
  of change, 65, 69
  of decision-making, 221
  destroying, 84
  of domineering boss, 75–76
  doubt vs., 25–26
  of failure, 59–60, 82
  faith, as antidote for, 84–85, 91
  as false belief, 80, 81
  of future, 61
  of humiliation, 9
  imagination and, 84, 86
  as pessimist, 91
  prayer to overcome, 75
  procrastination as, 110–11
  subconscious mind and, 80,
    83–84, 91
Feedback, effective communication
    and, 171, 172
Flux, state of, 63
Ford Motor Company, 64
Four-minute mile, courage and, 87
Fragility, of enthusiasm, 54, 57
Fulton, Robert, 96, 123

General Electric, 22, 193
Genius, 4, 63
Goal(s)
    achievement of, 5–6, 32–33
    action-based, 13, 189
    career, 5, 142
    conflicting wishes vs., 8
    dreams vs., 4, 5
    establishing, 3
    personal vs. team, 140
    Power of the Almighty and, 72
    setting realistic, 9–10
    setting, to break bad habit, 116
    seven steps to achievable, 12–14
    subconscious mind and, 132
    successful people and, 3, 53
    team career, 143
    time-related, 189
God, 138
    as boundless love, 74
    desire and, 72
    facing weaknesses and, 131, 134
    power of free choice and, 215
    time as gift from, 187
Goethe, Johann Wolfgang von, 214
The Golden Rule, 148
    as essence of religion, 137
    practice of, 175
    successful team leader and, 138
    true success and, 204
Goldstein, Susan and Sherman, 36
Good, 42–43, 175–76
Goodwill, 47, 59
    and law of mind, 174
    resolving conditions of others and, 78
    sincerity and, 203
    spiritual principle of forgiveness and,
        176–77
Gotcha, 182
Guidance, as replacement for criticism,
    152, 158
Guiding Principle, 57. See also Infinite
    Intelligence
Gund, Agnes, 165–66

Habit(s)
    acknowledging weakness, 112–13, 115

audible suggestion and, 113
of believing, 9, 29
breaking bad, 106, 108–12
building good, 107
coaching to change, 116
of expectancy, 7–8
forming new, 108, 109–10
in job performance, 106
old, and subconscious mind, 147
of speed over accuracy, 114–15
using behavior modification for,
    117
worry and, 81
Hall, Nicholas, 68–69
Handicap, 23
Harmony, 43–44, 176
Harriman, Edward, 99
Health, magnetic personality
    and, 46
Heart attack, psychosomatic, 73–74
Heart-to-heart talk, 183–84, 212
Hillel, 137–38
Hooper Steele, 100
Hotline, for Employee Assistance
    Program, 180
Huffington, Arianna, 30
Human nature
    appreciation and, 149
    hearing dictates of mind and, 165
    reading, for persuasion, 204
Humiliation, fear of, 9

Iacocca, Lee, 63–64, 65
Idea, 16, 103, 115, 168–69, 171
Illness, subconscious mind and,
    24–25
Imagination, 28, 105
    creativity and, 93–94, 97–98
    developing power of, 98–99
    fear and, 84, 86
    living role and, 9
    making real and, 214–15
    modern inventions and, 96
    Starbucks and, 94–95
    sustained, to remake world, 104
    using, for success, 216–17
    using, to rebuild life, 31

Increase, law of, 217
Inferiority, 16, 26
Infinite. *See also* Infinite Intelligence
　within, 216–17
　tuning into, 72
Infinite Intelligence, 57, 74
　principles of, 33
　solution to difficulty and, 177
　in subconscious, 72
　true place in life and, 213
Infinite Life, 74. *See also* Infinite
　Intelligence
Infinite Mind, 92
Infinite Power, 51, 64, 75
Infinite Spirit, responding to faith,
　74
Innovation, 64, 66, 99, 144
Inspiration
　Almighty and, 72
　of team members, 137
　victory from defeat and, 89–90
Instructions, to subconscious, 7–8
Interruptions
　from subordinates, 192–93
　telephone, 193–94
　visitors and, 194–95
Introspection, 9–10
Inventory, of accomplishments, 10–11

James, William, 39, 108, 149
Job(s)
　accepting change and, 142
　collaboration on, 144–45
　communication on, 162
　equanimity on, 76
　habits in, 106
　loss of, 5
　reducing fear/worry on, 80–81, 83
　training, team and, 140
Journal, time, 192
Joy, 55, 57, 59, 63
Judgment, refraining from hasty, 205

Karan, Donna, 65–66
Kimberly-Clark, 124
Kraft Foods, 220
Kullman, Ellen, 220

Language, destructive, 27–28
Law of substitution, 35–36, 74
Leadership
　ambition and, 127–28
　originality and, 133, 134
　qualities of great, 122–27
　subconscious mind and belief in,
　　130–31
　vision and, 126–27
Leaner, 55
Learning, 80, 221
Lee, Ivy, 189–90
Legend, Asian, 60–61
Leonard, Stew, 150
Life Force vs. negative thoughts, 31
Life script, 18–20
Lifetime Television, 67
Lifter, 55
Listening
　active, 139, 165–66, 172
　desire and, 202
　to find motivation, 206
　guidelines for improving, 166–67
Loss
　coming back from, 30–31
　of habit and grieving, 116
　of job, 5
　of self-esteem, 184, 185
　as test of courage, 89–90
　of trust, by team member, 141

Macy's Department Store, 204
Magnet(s), 44–45, 46
Magnetism, health and, 46
Mary Kay Cosmetics, 127–28, 155, 156
Master Architect, 97
Master list, 190, 191, 197
Master, of conceptive realm, 75, 79
Meditation
　Infinite Intelligence and, 74
　overcoming worry with, 75–77
　to train subconscious, 207
　on tuning into Infinite, 72
　unhappiness and, 184
Mental action, and fear, 83
Mental attitude, 8–9, 43
Mental confidence, 67

Mental image, 24
Mental kingdom, monarch of, 79
Mental law of attraction, 45–46
Mental state, inner, 173
Mentor, 39, 48, 50
Message, to subconscious, 8
Micromanaging, trust and, 113–14
Milton, John, 4
Mind, law of, 217
    materialization and, 9, 28
    projection and, 174
    relaxation and, 76–77
Mind-set, changing, 177
Mistakes, 47, 60
Modification, of products, 100–101
Moods. *See* Emotions
Motivation
    listening/empathizing to find, 206
    through peer recognition, 157–58
    of self, 139
    understanding others, for success, 205
Museum of Modern Art, 165–66

Negative suggestions. *See* Negative
    thoughts
Negative thoughts, 28, 65, 75
    dealing with immediately, 64
    Life Force and, 31
    refusing to identify with, 69
    remedy for, 33
    removing from the subconscious, 17
    supplanting with constructive, 71
Negative words
    as enemy of success, 27
    positive words vs., 21–22
    reversing, 38
Negativism, 31, 49, 57–58
Negativity
    blocking out, 89
    dealing with other's, 178–79, 186
North Jersey Limousine Service, 102

Objections, overcoming, 207–8
Observation
    improving powers of, 204–5
    saving money and, 100
    solving problems and, 105

Obstacle(s)
    commitments and, 133
    dyslexia as, 22–23
    overcoming, 3, 19–20, 30, 55, 117
    self-confidence and, 22–23
Odds, overcoming, 19
Opposition, goals and, 4
Optimism, 9, 28, 29–30, 37, 77

Pagels, Elaine, 5
Paradise Lost, 4
Paraphrase, as active listening
    skill, 166
Participation, 147, 218
Peluso, Michelle, 145–46
Pep talk, 21, 208, 210
Performance standards, team leaders
    and, 137
Perich, Sean, 122–23
Perseverance, goals and, 5
Persistence, 62–63
Personality, 44
    changing, 60
    dealing with negative, 178–79
    definition of, 39
    facial expressions and, 205–6
    ideal, 42
    magnetic, 40–41, 46
Persuasion
    art of, 198–99
    character-reading and, 204
    diplomacy, tact and, 206–7
    getting attention and, 200–201
    learning, 199
    pointing out value and, 206, 210
    thinking like salesperson and, 209
Pitney Bowes, 1–3, 104
Plan of action, 4
Positive thoughts
    as master thoughts, 64–65
    meditation on, 72
    negative vs., 21–22
    subconscious mind and, 37, 75–76,
        158
    substituting/replacing, for negative,
        17, 31
Potential, identifying, 10–11

Power(s)
  of the Almighty, 72
  enthusiasm and, 56–57
  of free choice, 215
  hidden, 10–11
  of imagination, 98–99
  Infinite, 51, 64, 75
  inner, 66, 132–33
  latent mind, 1
  of mind shadows, 74
  of observation, 204–5
  of self-confidence, 25, 28
  of suggestion, 33, 175
  will, and subconscious mind, 17
  word, 161
Praise, 153, 154–55, 159
Prayer, 95, 96
  for applying The Golden Rule, 175
  for equanimity on job, 76
  for guidance, 213
  relaxation and answered, 77–78
  unhappiness and, 184
  using, to overcome fear/worry, 75
Priorities, 189–91, 196
Problem, solving, 78, 102, 178
Procrastination, 110, 111–12
Professional organizations, membership
  in, 219
Proficiency, 25–26
Promotion, 23–24, 32–33
Promptness, drudgery of work and,
  111
Propositions, subconscious and, 16
Psychosomatic diseases, 73–74
Punishment vs. acceptance, 23–24
Purpose, oneness of, 11–12

Qualities, of attraction, 44–45, 131

Reactions, constructive vs.
  negative, 31
Recognition, 155, 157–58, 159
Reinforcement, positive, 152, 153,
  185
Rejection, of idea, 103
Relationships, 28–29, 209
Relaxation, 74, 76–77, 80

Remedy, for negative thinking, 33
Repetition, for self-esteem, 21
Resentment, 65
  growing in mind, 69
  as hindrance to advancement, 29, 32
  rejection and, 168–69
Resignation, replacing with
  positively, 37
Resilience, 59, 60, 64
Resolution, 54–55, 108–9
Resolve, 7–8, 57
Resources, 66
Respect, 20, 26, 29
Respite, to refresh mind, 79
Responsibility
  accepting, for team success, 138
  developing ability and, 133
  developing teammates through, 146
  for thoughts, 173, 174, 177
Results, 7–8
Return good for evil, 175–76
Rhimes, Shonda, 10
Rigidity, overcoming, 60
Risk, 139
Role model, 49
Roy, Rachel, 6–7

Sabotage, 32
Salespeople
  anticipating objections and, 207–8
  approaches used by successful,
    208–9
  ferreting out interests and, 205
Schultz, Howard, 94–95
Schwab, Charles, 189–90
Seattle, Washington, 94–95
Self-censorship, 99
Self-condemnation, criticism of others
  and, 174
Self-confidence, 1, 15–16, 26
  assertiveness training for, 185
  belief in self and, 18
  building, for team participation, 140
  handicaps and, 23
  leadership and, 124–25
  overcoming obstacles and, 21–23
  personal growth and, 142

power of, 25, 28
self-esteem from, 16–17
Self-defeating pattern, 116
Self-development, environment and, 68, 69–70
Self-direction, 34
Self-discovery, 66
Self-doubt, 68–69
Self-esteem, 1, 15, 26
creating, through fashion, 6
growth of, through success, 18
high, 16
letters of appreciation and, 157
loss of, 184, 185
nourishing, 20–21
planting in mind, through repetition, 21–22
from self-confidence, 16–17
unhappiness and, 184, 185
Self-flagellation, 24
Self-image, 18, 19–20, 26
Self-pity, 24
Self-reliance, 34–35
Selling
persuasion and, 198–99
quintessence of, 202
winning confidence and, 203
Sensitivity, to point of view, 139
Shadows of mind, 73, 74
Sincerity, goodwill and, 203
Skinner, B. F., 152
Slavery, overcoming, 19–20
Smith, Darwin, 124
Smith, Liz, 220
Socratic approach, 169
Soul, 94
Spellbinders, 203
Spirituality, stress release and, 80
Spiritual remedies, 72, 176–77
Stage fright, overcoming, 85
Starbucks man. See Schultz, Howard
State of mind, anger and, 173–74
Stew Leonard ABCD Award, 150
Straight-from-the-shoulder selling, 203
Straus, Nathan, 204
Strength, assessing for leadership, 130
Stress, ways to alleviate, 80–81

Subconscious mind
accepting change and, 144
activating, for confidence, 208, 210
adaptability and, 59–60
bad habits and, 108
belief and, 134
burdened with negativity, 76
conscious mind as pen for, 174–75
contradictions and, 16
creativity of, 33, 93
cure for heart trouble and, 74
directing to attain goals, 132
emotionalizing idea and, 16, 115
enhancing with innovation, 144–45
faith filtering down to, 74
fear and, 80, 91
habitual thinking and, 173
illness and, 24–25
inability to face problems and, 82
Infinite Intelligence in, 72
innovation and, 144
instructions to, 7–8
inventions and, 96
law of, 211–12, 221
leadership suggestions and, 130–31
meditation to train, 207
no fear and, 83–84
old habits and, 147
as one mind, 176–77
overcoming cancer and, 124
positive thoughts and, 75–76, 158
problem solving and, 69
programming, 26, 77, 166
projecting ideas and, 171
resisting domination with, 88, 92
right decision and, 216
self-confidence and, 125
superior knowledge vs., 207
team responsibility and, 138
time-oriented activities and, 191
untapped resources and, 24–25
visualization and, 99
willpower and, 17
word power and, 161
words of truth and, 72
Substitution, new technologies and, 101

Success
  attributes that lead to, 1, 15–16
  belief in self and, 124
  benefiting humanity and, 214
  career, 1, 119
  decision making and, 215–16
  delegation for, 128, 134
  enemy of, 27
  first step to, 221
  goals and, 3, 53
  The Golden Rule and, 204
  as incentive, 20–21
  increasing capacities for, 220–21
  log, 184–85
  mentoring and, 48, 50
  participation and, 147
  proficiency and, 25–26
  risks and, 60
  self-confidence and, 142
  self-esteem and, 18
  specializing in work and, 213–14
  teachers and, 202
  team leader and, 136–38, 147
  tenacity and, 11–12
  three steps to, 213–14
  thwarted by worry, 72
  understanding motivation and, 205
Success File, 156–57
Suggestion(s)
  power of, 33, 175
  rejecting with diplomacy, 168–69,
    172
Superiority, 182
Support team, help from, 81, 117
Supreme Intelligence. See Infinite
    Intelligence
Surgical team, as example of
    collaborative team, 136

Tact, 41
  effective persuasion and, 206–7
Talent vs. tenacity, 11–12
Tantrums, 181–82
Tea leaf, handling adversity and, 61–62
Team
  becoming great member of, 139–40
  career goals and, 143
  collaboration among members of,
    145–46
  commitment and, 135, 146
  concept, 141
  developing skills of, 137
  effort and job design, 144
  ideal, 136
  personal growth and, 142
  responsibility and, 146
  strengths and limitations of, 140
Team leader
  communication and, 137
  methods for success and, 136–38, 147
  special recognition and, 158
  from supervisor to, 143–44
  trust and, 141
Television production, 67
Tenacity, success from, 11–12
Tesla, Nikola, 96
TGIF. See Thank goodness it's Friday
Thank goodness it's Friday, 37
Think Big, 100–101
Thinking. See Thought(s)
Thought(s). See also Negative thoughts;
    Positive thoughts
  changing from fear to faith, 84–85, 91
  creative, 32, 64, 214
  destructive, 27
  emotion, reaction and action, 174
  feeding subconscious, 36, 158
  as magnets, 8–9
  master, 64, 75
Thought-enemies, 30
Thought-friends, 29
Time
  compared to infinite current, 187–88
  custom-build, 195–96
  goals and, 189
  power to control, 187–88
Time management, 187
  delegating and, 195–96
  essential ingredient of, 190–91
  establishing goals and, 189
  handling interruptions and, 192–93
  saying no and, 196, 197
  time journal and, 191–92
  time robbers and, 192–94, 195

Traits, 40, 41–42, 43, 44
Travelocity, 145–46
TravelSmith, 201
Trust, 20
    as basis for relationship, 147
    loss of, by team leader, 141
    micromanaging and, 113–14
Truth, 23–24, 131–32, 175
Two-way street, communication as, 171–72
Tylenol, recall of, 125

Unhappy people, dealing with, 183, 184–86
Universe, change and, 63
U.S. Postal Service, 103

Vancouver, British Columbia, 95
Visibility, 217–19, 222
Vision
    leadership and, 126–27
    marketing strategy and, 104
    of team, 137
Visualization, 36–37, 38
    for character qualities, 131–32
    real estate and, 95
    of results, 7–8
    Starbucks and, 94–95
    vivid, 99
Volunteer, visibility in organization and, 218–19

Walgreen, Charles, R., 126
Walgreens Drugstore Company, 126

Walk, to alleviate stress, 80
Weaknesses, 131, 132, 134
Weinstein, Jeff, 195–96
Welch, Jack, 193
Willpower, subconscious mind and, 17
Wise man, 61, 77
Wong, Andrea, 67
Word(s)
    positive vs. negative, 21–22
    producing results from, 161
    thought expressed as, 177–78
    of truth, 72
Work
    detail vs. sales, 11
    enthusiasm for, 52–53, 55, 56, 57
    experience, 10
    lack of, experience, 55
    procrastination vs., 111
    specializing in, for success, 213–14
    unhappy people and, 183–86
Workload, analyzing for delegation, 195–96
Worry, 71, 83
    conquering, 72–73
    cure for, 86
    as false belief, 80, 81
    habit of, 81
    overcoming, with meditation/prayer, 75–77
    reducing on job, 80–81
    shadows of mind and, 73

"You Made My Day," as message of thanks, 157–58

About the Author

Joseph Murphy, born on May 20, 1898, in a small town in the County of Cork, Ireland, was enrolled in the National School, where he excelled. Encouraged to study for the priesthood, he was accepted as a Jesuit seminarian.

However, by the time he reached his late teen years, he began to question the Catholic orthodoxy of the Jesuits and he withdrew from the seminary. As his goal was to explore new ideas and gain new experiences, a goal he could not pursue in Catholic-dominated Ireland, he left his family to go to America.

He arrived at the Ellis Island Immigration Center with only five dollars in his pocket. His first project was to find a place to live. He was fortunate to locate a rooming house where he shared a room with a pharmacist who worked in a local drugstore.

His knowledge of English was minimal as Gaelic was spoken both in his home and at school, so like most Irish immigrants, Murphy worked as a day laborer, earning enough to keep fed and housed.

He and his roommate became good friends, and when a job opened up at the drugstore where his friend worked, he was hired to be an assistant to the pharmacist. He immediately enrolled in a school to study pharmacy, and qualified as a full-fledged pharmacist. He eventually purchased the drugstore and for the next few years ran a successful business.

When the United States entered World War II, Murphy enlisted in the U.S. Army and was assigned to work as a pharmacist in a medical unit. While in the Army, he renewed his interest in religion and began to read extensively about various religious beliefs. After his discharge, he chose not to return to his career in pharmacy. He traveled extensively and took courses at several universities both in the United States and abroad.

From his studies, he became enraptured by the various Asian religions and went to India to learn about them in depth. He extended his studies to the great philosophers from ancient times until the present.

The one person who most influenced Murphy was Dr. Thomas Troward, who was a judge as well as a philosopher, doctor, and professor. Judge Troward became Joseph's mentor. From him he not only learned philosophy, theology, and law but also was introduced to mysticism and particularly to the Masonic order. Murphy became an active member of this order and over the years rose in the Masonic ranks to the 32nd degree in the Scottish Rite.

Upon his return to the United States, he chose to become a minister. As his concept of Christianity was not traditional and indeed ran counter to most of the Christian denominations, he founded his own church in Los Angeles. He attracted a small number of congregants, but it did not take long for his message of optimism and hope to attract many men and women to his church.

Dr. Murphy was a proponent of the New Thought movement, which advocated combining a metaphysical, spiritual, and pragmatic approach to the way we think and live, to uncover the secret of attaining what we truly desire. We can do all these things only as we have found the law and worked out the understanding of the law, which God seemed to have written in riddles in the past.

Over the years other churches joined with Dr. Murphy in developing an organization called the Divine Science Federation, which acts as an umbrella for all Divine Science Churches.

Murphy's local Church of Divine Science grew so large that he had to rent the Wilshire Ebell Theater, a former movie house. His services were so well attended that even this venue could not always accommodate all who wished to attend. To reach the vast numbers of people who wanted to hear his message, Dr. Murphy created a weekly radio talk show, which eventually reached an audience of more than a million listeners.

He taped his lectures and radio programs, and the initial success that he saw in marketing the cassettes started a new venture to increase his outreach. The tapes featured lectures explaining biblical texts and provided meditations and prayers for his listeners. He also started to publish pamphlets and small books of his inspirational material.

As a result of his books, tapes, and radio broadcasts, Dr. Murphy's reputation grew exponentially and he was invited to lecture throughout the United States, Europe, and Asia. In addition to religious matters, he spoke on the historical values of life, on the art of wholesome living, and on the teachings of great philosophers—from both the Western and Asian cultures. In all his lectures, he emphasized the importance of understanding the power of the subconscious mind and the life-principles based on belief in the one God, the "I AM."

He wrote more than thirty books. His most famous book, *The Power of the Unconscious Mind*, first published in 1963, became an immediate bestseller. Millions of copies have been sold and continue to be sold all over the world in a wide variety of languages.

Dr. Murphy died in December 1981. His wife, Dr. Jean Murphy, continued his ministry until her death.

About the Editor

This book was compiled and edited by **Dr. Arthur R. Pell**, author of more than fifty books and hundreds of articles on management, human relations, and self-improvement. In addition to his own writings, Dr. Pell has edited and updated many of the classics on human potential, including Dale Carnegie's *How to Win Friends and Influence People*, Napoleon Hill's *Think and Grow Rich*, Joseph Murphy's *The Power of Your Subconscious Mind*, James Allen's *As a Man Thinketh*, Yoritomo-Tashi's *Common Sense*, and works by Orison Swett Marden, Julia Seton, and Wallace D. Wattles.